Mary Jo Tobin is a tireless and selfless advocate for animals in New York City, and this book reflects those efforts. Her enthusiasm is infectious, and it's gratifying to see formerly homeless and neglected animals find caring homes through her efforts.

-Joe Pentangelo
Animal Cruelty Investigator

I met Mary Jo when I volunteered at the very first adoption event and have been at almost every one since. She welcomed me with open arms, and we have become good friends. It's awesome to see how people can get behind a great cause. Even when the turnout is 'bad' we still have twenty to twenty-five dogs, cats, puppies, and kittens . . . and even rabbits . . . finding new homes and being saved from potentially being euthanized. Mary Jo's efforts, love and concern for these animals is overwhelming.

-Robert Machi
Dog Behavioral Therapist & Trainer Bark Busters Home Dog Training

LOVE
WANTED

Jeffrey,
Happy Birthday!
Enjoy the Book —

M. J.

LOVE WANTED

True Tails of Love, Loss and Redemption

Mary Jo Tobin

TATE PUBLISHING & Enterprises

TATE PUBLISHING
& Enterprises

Tate Publishing is committed to excellence in the publishing industry. Our staff of highly trained professionals, including editors, graphic designers, and marketing personnel, work together to produce the very finest books available. The company reflects the philosophy established by the founders, based on Psalms 68:11,

"THE LORD GAVE THE WORD AND GREAT WAS THE COMPANY OF THOSE WHO PUBLISHED IT."

If you would like further information, please contact us:
1.888.361.9473 | www.tatepublishing.com
TATE PUBLISHING & Enterprises, LLC | 127 E. Trade Center Terrace
Mustang, Oklahoma 73064 USA

To my Buckwheat and my Gallagher, and all the rest of my furry family, my deepest thanks for giving me twenty years of unconditional love, laughs, companionship and memories and for showing me how important it is to have a furry friend or two in my life! I've been so blessed to have had the pleasure of being a part of your lives and for this I will always cherish and love you all. Your paw-prints will forever be on my heart and in my soul.

ACKNOWLEDGEMENTS

Over 600 pets have been placed in loving homes since beginning this mission in November of 2004. This kind of success doesn't just happen. It takes an enormous love of animals and the cooperation, hard work and shared vision of many people. It is impossible to mention everyone here and, to anyone who has participated but isn't mentioned by name, you know that you have my deepest appreciation for all that you have done to help our really important cause.

The very first person I want to mention is Chase Reynolds Ewald. Without Chase's strong encouragement for the past ten years to write a book, I would never have had the confidence to think that this was something I could actually accomplish. Chase seemed to think I had what it took to do it and gave me enough assurance and support to make me finally believe I could. She took tons of time out from her super busy life to help me with edits and ideas. I will be forever grateful to her.

Then there's my husband, Sal Katzos. He deserves tons of thanks for his patience with me during the past year and a half. In addition to opening my own real estate office, I have spent endless hours away from home doing animal rescue work, writing and editing this book and promoting and hosting these events. Together we have spent countless weeks and tons of money fostering litter after litter of kittens. He played a huge role in bottle feeding and socializing these little boogers, making those times fun and memorable! He even built them cool kitty-condos out of boxes from the supermarket. All of these efforts have taken an enormous chunk of time and energy from our home life. He's been a great sport through it all, always saying the right thing to keep me going no matter how tired or overwhelmed I felt. Without his love and support, I would never have accomplished so many things in such a short period of time! He was also very valuable to me with the editing process. His grammar is far superior to mine.

Next are my parents. I know that I have gotten my intense love of animals from my Dad. Some of my earliest memories include seeing him spend Sunday afternoons feeding and loving the dirty, mangy stray dogs on the Brooklyn waterfront where he worked. Those dogs loved him and appreciated every kind gesture he showed them. Those powerful images will forever live warmly in my heart. From my Mom I have learned that life is not about what people can do for you but rather what you can do for people, or in my case pets! Thanks Mom and Dad for setting such wonderful examples. Not everyone is lucky enough to have role models like you guys!

Many members of my family have been drawn into this mission. My sisters, Susan Rocchio and Monica Savarese both lent assistance in different ways. Susie played a crucial role in my office. She helped with the phones and greeted the almost constant flow of walk-in animal lovers. She spent tons of time answering any animal related questions that came her way, always with a full heart and plenty of enthusiasm! She is a mini-me in so many ways and I love her to death! Monica came to the first handful of events and took the most awesome, professional quality photos, which I will always treasure. Then there are my nephews, Matthew Tobin, John Savarese and Kevin Savarese. Matt, though not a big animal lover, he read my entire book and helped me with the initial phase of the editing process, which was no easy task. He made a tedious job fun and entertaining. John made the coolest fliers for many of the events. They were witty and eye-catching. Kevin was my "junior photographer" and captured some really cool moments of the events in progress.

Then there is Pat Downs. Pat was my biggest supporter and true partner for the first year. She gave her time, money, energy and support and cheerfully accompanied me on many zany rescue missions. Together we accomplished truly amazing things. I would also like to express my deep appreciation to the really wonderful folks at the Animal Care and Control of NYC; Mary Martin, Richard Gentles, Latisha Townsend, Sabrina James, Joseph Calegari, Joyce Clemmons and everyone else who has made working with them an absolute pleasure and a tremendous win-win situation for us all. Claire Balchumus from North Shore Animal League is someone that I will always be indebted to for making sure that our first event was a huge success. Without Claire's support and intervention that first day, none of this would have happened. Also I'd like to express my sincerest gratitude to the many other kind folks at North Shore Animal League for helping coordinate our events and for graciously providing the transportation for the Animal Care and Control pets. Without North Shore's support of our events we'd be nowhere. I'd also like to thank the wonderful folks, especially Fr. John Farrell and Todd Schultz, at The Christ Church, for so generously opening their grounds to us for over a year and have playing an integral role in our success.

Like I said, without volunteers our mission could never have been realized to the extent it has. Thanks to the help of people like my sister-in-law, Judy Savarese and Ruth Bedell, who adopted Lili from me, we have far exceeded any numbers we could have ever imagined. Judy and Ruth work non-stop to help promote these events. Judy tirelessly posts fliers everywhere she possibly can, even in the coldest of weather. Ruth is a walking tribute to our cause. She brings her adorable Lili everywhere she goes and anyone who admires her is given either a flier for our next event or my business card and told to contact me. There is also Karen Bladykis, MD, who not only volunteers to help at every event, but she has taken on three more dogs since meeting me. Karen is a remarkable woman who never turns away an animal in need, regardless of how much extra work, money and heartbreak it may cost her.

I owe an enormous amount of gratitude and love to my best buddy, Phil Zarr, who I have dragged all over town in the coldest of weather posting fliers with me late at night. We'd be walking with frozen fingers and numb toes, but Phil's gift of being a wonderful storyteller always managed to keep me laughing, somehow making this daunting job fun! I can't thank Robert Machi of Bark Busters Home Dog Training enough. Robert has donated many, many hours of his time and expertise in helping potential adopters make the right choice. He has gone above and beyond in providing sound advice and counseling over the phone to anyone facing challenges with their new pooches. Then there are the volunteers who, in addition to working hard at the events, come and pick up fliers to post and distribute to the local shops and vets, Margie Nichols, Carolanne Mahoney, Carla O'Neil, Marina O'Neil and so many others. They save me so much leg-work and for that I am very grateful.

I also have to thank my good pal John McKeon who has dubbed me "the Wordsmith." John has been a long-time, wonderful friend and continual source of encouragement and support. His patience, intelligence, hard-earned wisdom and kind heart have inspired, strengthened and helped me be a better, more patient person.

So many rescues would not have happened if it hadn't been for the relationship I have with my best friend, Joanne Marini. Joanne and I have been through unbelievable challenges together through the years and she is truly the best friend that anyone could ever hope or pray to be blessed with! She works for a very busy vet's office and together, through countless phone calls and lots of networking, we have kept probably close to seventy-five pets from being brought to the shelter.

Lastly, I have to thank Janey Hayes of Tate Publishing for recognizing that I had stories that needed and deserved to be told and for offering me the opportunity to work with Tate Publishing and its wonderful staff on this really special project.

As Hillary Clinton said, "It takes a village," and I am so blessed to be part of a village like the one the people of Bay Ridge, Brooklyn comprise!

FOREWORD

THIS BOOK IS one woman's story about success. Motivational and heroic, Mary Jo's journey is a must read for all those who want to get off of the sidelines, get involved and make a difference but may not know how to get started.

It is estimated that between six and eight million cats and dogs enter shelters each year costing communities millions of tax dollars. Although animal shelters try valiantly to cope with the consequences of this surplus of pets, sadly, many of them will lose their lives simply because they were not lucky enough to be adopted.

It is abundantly clear to those of us who labor in city animal shelters that those government agencies will never be able to end pet homelessness without the support of dedicated community members. Unfortunately, many people don't understand the complexity of the issues, and others simply avoid the problem entirely. They assume that no one person could possibly make a significant difference. Fortunately for the hundreds of homeless pets in New York City, Mary Jo Tobin decided that no matter how complex or how enormous the problem, she had to get involved.

Mary Jo rejected all the excuses and reasons not to act. She did not allow herself the luxury of playing the blame game; bad owners, bad shelters etc. Instead she developed an adoption program that has, to date, resulted in hundreds of lives saved.

Mary Jo receives no compensation for what she does and has donated more than $10,000 of her own money to organize, plan and implement fourteen pet adoption events. With many more adoption "days" on the calendar, Mary Jo's legion of volunteers continue to plan, organize and carry out each event. She has been so successful at getting the "word out" that there is often a long line of people waiting to adopt when the dogs and cats arrive.

In addition to the lives saved, Mary Jo has brought joy and love into the homes of hundreds of people in Brooklyn and the surrounding areas. We are very grateful to Mary Jo for the work she has done to support Animal Care & Control of NYC and for the hundreds of lives she has saved. It is our hope that after reading her touching and inspiring stories that you will be compelled to become part of the growing community of people that make a difference for homeless pets.

Mary Martin and Richard P. Gentles
Animal Care & Control of New York City

PICTURE IT, BROOKLYN, 1969

SINCE I WAS very young, I have loved dogs. When I was in the second grade my father brought home a black Scottie named Angus. I spent hours in the backyard with Angus sharing Milkbones—one for him, one for me. Unfortunately my mom did not share this love for Angus; instead she was filled with quite another feeling—rage! What was he thinking? She had four kids and needed a dog like she needed a broken leg! Back in those days she had no clothes dryer, no microwave, a baby in diapers and a husband who worked seven days a week, twelve hours a day! She was, to say the very least, not a happy camper. And as any smart man knows, when Mom is not a happy camper, no one is a happy camper—and most of all, Dad. Before I knew it, my wonderful little Scottie was gone. I was so sad—heartbroken, really. But now, looking back, I understand why my mom felt the way she did. Four kids is an awful lot of work. Being Irish immigrants, she and my dad had no family here to help them. She worked to the bone raising us and keeping up with laundry, ironing (all those pleated catholic uniform skirts!), shopping, cooking and cleaning. But at the time, boy, was I disappointed.

When I was a 1st and 2nd grader, on Sunday afternoons my dad would take me down to the waterfront where he worked. He was head of security for a pier in Brooklyn, and there were countless stray dogs living on the pier that he fed and took care of. I loved going with him and looked forward to those visits. I will never forget how the dogs would recognize his car as he approached the gate and run up to meet him. He would roll down the window and the dogs would jump up and kiss him all over his face. I delighted in this! These dogs were always filthy from living on the docks, and my hands would be black and grimy by the time I had finished petting them, but I didn't care! The reason for my dad's trip to the pier on those Sunday afternoons was to bring the dogs some leftovers from our Sunday dinners. These dogs were well fed, being served roast beef, mashed potatoes and gravy every Sunday. I could see that my dad was as crazy about these dirty little creatures as I was. I have to believe that I got my intense love of animals from my dad.

After Angus, I vowed that I would get a dog as soon as I possibly could. That dog did come many years later, but it took my getting married and buying my own house. He arrived on Christmas Eve of 1986, as a gift from my then husband, Chris. The most beautiful little black Lab mix puppy was in a wicker basket with an enormous red bow around his neck with a little note saying, "Hello, my name is Sinbad." Well, hello Sinbad! I was excited beyond words! But the name Sinbad had to go. I renamed him Buckwheat. This was truly the most wonderful gift I have ever received and never in my life will I receive a gift as wonderful and as memorable as my Buckwheat—I still miss him so much. He died on October 26, 1996, just shy of his tenth birthday.

I was so excited and instantly overprotective of him. We brought him to my parent's house that night for our traditional Christmas Eve Celebration. I knew I was insane about him when he peed all over my nice Christmas outfit as I sat on my mom's couch and I just laughed. My Buckwheat quickly meant the world to me. I took him everywhere with me. He was, in my eyes, the most beautiful little fellow on earth. He looked like a black golden retriever, silky and shiny and always well behaved. His disposition was such that I could trust him with everyone. Even the peeping Tom who lurked outside my apartment window wasn't worried about him. When I happened to stumble upon this creep in the courtyard one evening looking in my windows while it was pouring rain, Buckwheat thought it was wonderful to have a visitor and ran down the alleyway wagging his tail like crazy, as if to say, "Hey, where ya going, come back, pet me, what's your rush?"

After three years, my marriage suddenly dissolved but my love for Buck only got stronger. My first divorce was a very drawn out process.

We had to sell our home and, at twenty-six years old, I was distraught that my husband had left me for a "younger" woman. I look back now and laugh but at the time I felt so old—twenty-six and divorced. The year was 1989 and in New Jersey a few people had recently committed suicide by carbon monoxide poisoning in their garages. "Yes, that's it." I thought one evening as I sat feeling sorry for myself. That would be how I would "get even" with my soon-to-be ex. I would commit suicide in our two car garage. I would have a few glasses of wine and then go down, bringing along a book to help pass the time while I waited for the carbon monoxide to work its magic. But then, I looked at Buckwheat. Who in the world would take as good care of my little man as I could? How would he survive without his mommy? So, Buckwheat saved my life.

If there can be a lucky one in a divorce, I guess it was me. I got custody of my beloved dog. In my mind, it was like winning the lottery. I could not have imagined Chris keeping him! He could have all the china, the TV, the VCR and the new car we bought—but my sweet little mutt, Buckwheat? Chris's new girlfriend was a woman with five cats and after a short while would not "allow" him to continue seeing the dog—for a while we had "shared custody." I must say I am grateful to her for that.

Being newly divorced and in a strange apartment, I was afraid I'd feel so lonely. I had never lived alone before. I was one of five children and moved from my parent's home to my married home. Almost four years had passed since I had gotten Buckwheat and in my eyes he had become almost human. He was my best friend. He licked my tears away through that awful divorce and, with him by my side, I never felt lonely. He truly was my buddy—my very best buddy. In between being married, I would have the choice between going to a bar with my friends to hang out and look for Mr. Right or staying in and enjoying what had now become my "lovely" apartment with Buckwheat and a glass of wine—it was a no-brainer! So we'd rent a good movie and curl up on the couch together. Those were wonderful, simple times.

I did meet many interesting men during this period of my life and my biggest criteria in deciding who was a keeper was how they reacted to Buckwheat and how Buckwheat reacted to them. One was allergic and wanted me to get rid of him. Next! Another one was a very handsome fellow who was a real doll but certainly not an animal lover. He actually looked me in the eye and asked, "How long do you think he has left?" to which I replied, "Longer than you." And the list went on.

I had become a little over the top when it came to my dog—who, by the way, had no idea he was a dog. I never told him. Just like when I had him neutered, I told him he was having his tonsils taken out . . . the way I see it, a little white lie never hurt anyone, right? In my mind, then and now, there are worse things to be than over the top in love with my pet or in my current life *pets:* three dogs, four cats, and always something being fostered.

GALLAGHER ARRIVES, BUCKWHEAT DEPARTS, MOW MOW IS BORN

I'D LIKE TO share some background on my current animal situation so that you understand a bit better who I am and what my home life is like. When God closes a door he opens a window, right? That is kind of how things went with me and Gallagher. God took away my Buckwheat six months *after* he gave me Gallagher. There are no coincidences in life, and over time I realized that when people say all things happen for a reason, it is the truest statement ever uttered. I have to believe that Gallagher was purposely put in my path to help ease the pain of losing my Buckwheat.

Gallagher is the greatest love of my life! I almost feel guilty saying this because I was crazy about my Buckwheat, but the relationship was very different and Buckwheat was always sick and a difficult dog to own because of his chronic illnesses. My Gallagher, on the other hand, has been a pure pleasure, blessed with excellent health. I am absolutely crazy about her. Trying to put into words what she means to me is simply impossible. She is that once in a lifetime dog that some people are lucky enough to experience! I consider myself to be enormously lucky. Our relationship certainly didn't start out that way. I have had my Gallagher for over ten years now. The time has just gone too fast. Each day I see her getting older. The older she gets, the more I realize that my time with her is less and less. This breaks my heart because she is *the best*. No other way to describe her . . . simply *the best*.

Gallie, as she is known, is a gorgeous Husky, Lab and Shepherd mix. I was lucky enough to find her wandering during the height of the evening rush hour on a bustling avenue that had four lanes of very busy traffic. I was walking with my dear friend Joan Gallagher. We'd gotten off the subway four stops early so we could walk the streets of Brooklyn to get a little exercise. Since we were forever battling the bulge, when the weather permitted we would walk. As we strolled along, deep in office gossip, I noticed this beautiful dog just about to commit doggie suicide by attempting to walk out into oncoming traffic. "Come here, puppy dog," I yelled in a high pitched voice. Thank God I was able to attract her attention. I grabbed the miserably small length of thin chain that was around her neck. No joke this chain was made for a toy poodle, and it had hanging about a foot of excess for someone to hold it. I grabbed onto it, and prayed that the dog would stay with me. No problem, she instantly felt good with me and was more than happy to walk along with us. Joan, who I always affectionately called Gallagher because we worked with a bunch of other women named Joan, and I walked up and down the local streets looking to see if there were signs for a lost dog. We stopped everyone we met as they were coming home from work to see if they knew the dog. We rang bells at the local apartment buildings to see if anyone knew the dog. We stopped every dog owner we met along our way to see if they recognized the dog. No luck, no one knew this big, ninety plus pound beauty.

I was lucky enough to have the dog's complete cooperation for our long thirty-block walk to my house. She was a delight to walk, and I was in complete amazement at how well behaved and beautiful she was. On our way, Joan left us at her corner and continued on her way home. I still had another twelve blocks to walk with my new find. Along the way, I continued to ask people if they recognized her or if they had seen any signs for a missing dog; no luck.

When we arrived at my house, Buckwheat was a perfect gentleman, as usual. It never occurred to me that aggression was something I needed to fear because this dog was so excellent on our way home. I walked her with that skimpy chain, and we had met other dogs along the way and she was a gem. So, what transpired next was a complete shock. I put a better leash and collar on her and began to walk both her and Buckwheat around the block, as I did with Buck every night when I came home from work. As we rounded the corner, the new dog decided to attack my little man! I panicked! I couldn't stop them. Then along came this casually dressed man with a knapsack hanging off his shoulder, and I begged him to please take one of the dogs so I could separate them. His name was Sal, and he was more than willing to help me with my dilemma. What's more, we ended up getting married a few years later.

I finally got the two dogs apart and calm. I felt awful. I felt like I put my Bucky at risk by taking in this beast. I was mad at her. What an absolute bully this dog was. I would not put up with that. She had to go. I had to find her owner or a new home. She was mean to my boy, and no one is mean to my boy and gets away with it! The next day, I made seventy-five fliers and posted them on poles in the area where I had found her. Then I called all the vets in the area asking if any of their clients had lost a dog. I called the police precincts and the local dog shelter—again, no luck. I placed ads in the paper for a found dog. At this point, I tried to get my younger sister to take her. She tried, but the dog was too strong for her and she couldn't control her. She was terrible on a leash and pulled like a sled dog in training. I could barely control her, let alone my poor sister who only weighed thirty pounds more than the dog. Then I tried to get my brother and his wife to take her. She would not stop digging in their yard. She ruined all their flowers. So she was returned to me—again! I couldn't believe that this beast was the same dog that had walked so politely all the way home with me that first night.

By this point, she needed a name. I decided on Gallagher, after my friend Joan. Joan didn't consider this *the honor* that I considered it to be and started yelling at me, "I can't believe that you're naming a freaking dog after me . . ." To which I responded, "To me this is an honor. It is like me naming my first born after you and, besides, she has your personality . . . She is the toughest thing I have ever met, so the name stays!" So began my life with Gallagher. No one would take her. I had not one response to my signs and it was becoming evident that she was staying. Buckwheat was okay with this but not thrilled. Gallagher, however, continued to be a terrible to him. One hot June night she even attacked him for a cookie. She bit his ear and my fingers when I tried to stop her! She was skating on thin ice. During this time, I started to date Sal, the guy who helped me with her the first night. It turned out that he was newly divorced—as was I—and he was my neighbor's son, temporarily living next door. He was not someone I ever expected to get involved with—totally not my type. But Gallagher brought us together. He was crazy about her and Buck and turned out to be as big of a dog lover as I was, and he was into cats as well. I hadn't discovered the world of cats yet. That came a few years later.

Long story made short, from May till October, Gallagher misbehaved, always giving Buckwheat a hard time. She was an Alpha dog and up until then, I had no idea those kinds of dogs even existed. I kept thinking about what a fine act she put on for me on our long walk home that first night—perfectly behaved. The truth was she couldn't have been more unruly on a leash. She was just smart, playing me for a fool that day! The reality of it was that walking Gallagher built up my leg muscles. She had absolutely no manners and was extremely difficult to control. She hated—not just disliked, but hated—other dogs, and even if they were a block away, she would go insane trying to get away from me to get them. I wasn't happy with this dog at all. What's more, there would be no more dog run visits for Buck because of this anti-social Alpha Witch!

Six months later, in October of 1996, Buckwheat began to cough. It was a bizarre cough, very raspy and deep. I took him to the vet, where he was given some medicine and I was told it was something that was common in Labs. Okay, fair enough, I thought. I would give him the medicine, and he would be fine in no time. No such luck. As the evening progressed, Buckwheat began to throw up clear liquid. It went on all through the night. It literally didn't stop. Every five minutes, he would throw up. I was getting frantic. I sat on the floor with him all night, crying. What was going on? Finally, at 5:30 am, I called my mom and asked her to drive us to the emergency vet. I then took Buckwheat outside to wait for her. He immediately did his business at the curb.

What a good boy, he never had an accident in the house, ever! He was the best little fellow, and I was so in love with him. He wasn't very old, not ten yet. I tried to stay calm. Then I realized Buck had bubbles of water coming out of his nose. What was going on? I was scared to death now. Moments later I realized that his body was actually bloated looking, like he was retaining water. Now I was terrified. Sadly, Buckwheat was dead within two hours. He had something called Mega-Esophagus, and he was drowning right before my eyes.

I sat with him as they gave him the first shot to relax him. He tried to stand up, almost startled. I was inconsolable, sitting on the floor of this cold, smelly emergency vet's office by myself with this ice cold, very matter of fact, young vet putting my best friend in the world to sleep! This vet lacked empathy and compassion, which only compounded the terrible feelings I was experiencing at that moment. As Buck tried to stand up after the first shot, I said to him what I had said to him every night of his life, "Okay, little man, it's time to go sleepy." Within moments he was gone. It was quick, but it seemed like an eternity to me. The vet then handed me Buckwheat's orange bandana and his neon green collar, and that is all that I left with, that and a bill for $1,500 for a dog that was now dead! How I managed to sign the receipt is still something I can't figure out. I was hysterical, brokenhearted and blinded by tears.

I went home and cried the entire day. My eyes were swollen and purple. Sal tried so hard to say the right things but there were no right things to be said. I was destroyed. My older sister sent me a dozen roses, and when the tenants upstairs heard my wailing and what had happened, they too sent me flowers and a card. My parents didn't know what to say or do for me. They, too, were heartbroken. My dad loved Buck, and he was their first "grandchild." Everyone was in mourning, but I was truly a mess. I called my ex-husband, who had given me Buckwheat. He was so sad when I told him what happened that he showed up at my house that night with an 8 ½ x 14 framed picture of Buckwheat that we used to have over our couch. In the divorce, I got the dog, and he got the picture. But now he was kind enough to bring me what was our favorite framed picture of our little man. I was very grateful for that, and all these years later his picture is above my couch.

Buck died on a Sunday morning. I didn't go to work until Thursday. I couldn't because I couldn't stop crying. It was impossible for me to have a conversation with anyone without crying. I had never lost anyone or anything that was that close to me before. I know I am very lucky to have been thirty-three years old and to be able to say that! But that didn't take the pain away. I was wrecked. Even more upsetting to me was that each time I'd think of Buck, I would immediately flash back to our last moments together, in that cold, miserable emergency vet's office! Why couldn't I think of our nights sitting on the couch or playing at the dog run? Instead, I was tormented by those rotten images of Buck's heart stopping, and him slowly slumping onto the cold floor of the cage. The end was ugly, not anything that I would have planned, if I could have planned such a thing.

The response I got from my immediate boss when I returned to work was this: "What's the big deal, you have another dog." Almost as if to say, "Get over it." I was really upset and explained that my dogs were like my kids and, that as far as I was concerned, I had just lost my son. I got through my explanation without any tears and then went to the ladies room and cried my heart out. This multi-millionaire had no idea what he was missing out on in life. He had no love for animals, and to him they were just that, animals.

As time went by, I began to beat myself up for taking in Gallagher and allowing her to impose on Buckwheat's last six months of life. I was filled with guilt. I was upset with myself for introducing another dog into our last six months together. Had I known that was all we had left, I would have taken a leave of absence and made sure I spent all my waking hours with my boy doing things he loved, like going to the dog run. Boy, was I feeling bad for Buckwheat and resentful of Gallagher. I decided that I was angry with her and needed to find her a home. My sister, Monica, not a dog lover at all, kept telling me that Gallie-girl was a great dog and that I should keep her. I didn't agree. I wanted her out. I wanted to find her a home. She had been mean to my Buck and because of that I couldn't continue to house her. So, once again, I tried to find her a home. Again, no luck! What was going on? She was gorgeous, housebroken and learning manners. Why did no one want her? Now, looking back, I realize it was a lucky thing for us both that I found her at that point in my life when I wasn't a pro at finding homes for pets—what we call re-homing. We would have truly missed out on the best relationship imaginable.

After about a month of unforgiving, relentless grief, I decided to give Gallagher a chance. It wasn't her fault that she was a big, bossy dog. It wasn't her fault that I found her and brought her home. None of it was her fault. She was who she was. Her personality was growing on me, and we began to make strides in teaching her manners. She was becoming less and less aggressive with other dogs and was really becoming a good girl. One day at a time, that's how we took it. And now, I cannot imagine my life without her.

Gallagher at this point is at least eleven years old. Each day, I can see her getting a little older, a little slower and a little closer to leaving me. I can't bear the thought. Even as I write this, my eyes are stinging with tears. That is the downside to having animals . . . they just don't last long enough! We make a point of enjoying her each and every day. Sal and I understand that our time with her is short and only getting shorter, so we go out of our way to make sure her time is special, comfortable and happy.

Like so many pet owners, we have special, silly names that we call her. She is first and foremost Mommy. We call her Mommy because she is just that, a real Momma. We have six other animals, and she is the referee. We can always count on Gallagher to give us a heads up when the cats have had enough of our overzealous puppy, Nuggie, licking their faces. The poor cats sit meowing like crazy while allowing Nuggie to lick their faces uncontrollably. Nuggie loves cats so much that she goes crazy over them and they are good sports—to a point. After a while they will slowly raise their paws, which are equipped with very sharp nails. This is the point that Gallagher begins to show what kind of Momma/Babysitter she is. As soon as a feline paw gets raised, Gallagher is squeaking and growling to let us know what's up. Despite her age and her bad legs, somehow she manages to get herself up to protect the pup, in record time. She will go over and head butt the cats out of the way, or she will gently chase them into another room and make sure they stay away from her Nuggie. When we are home and she does this, we always tell her to relax. Some nights I will be standing doing dishes and these one sided love-fests between the puppy and one of the cats will start taking place, Gallagher will start with her squeaking, and I always say to her, "Relax, Gal, I'm the Mommy when I'm home, relax!" And being the smart lady that she is, she understands and relaxes!

The other day I came in from a very long day at work and found my husband just finishing up a martini. He is particularly funny after a martini or two. As I stood there chatting with him about my day and some of the annoying people I encountered, the love-fest started up, and as I began to tell Gallagher to relax, that I am home and that I'm the Mommy, my husband broke out with, "I know, I was telling her before to relax, *that I'm the Mommy . . .*"

Another name we call Gallagher is Mommy-Knows, and that is simply because she knows. She knows who's normal, and who's not quite normal. She has the most amazing ability to discern who is wacky or drunk. Whenever I walk her, if anyone approaches and tries to chat with us—someone who's not all there—he is out of luck. Gallie will not allow him to chat with us. Only sane, normal people are permitted.

There is a very short, eccentric fellow named Ike in the neighborhood who loves "Gal-a-her," as he calls her. For years now, each time he sees her from across the street he gets giddy with excitement and these bizarre squeals start to come out of his mouth. He's a nice guy, a big dog lover, but a little different. "Gal-a-her" will have none of it. Poor guy can't get within 10 feet of her. She immediately starts lunging—showing her teeth and getting all ugly with him. I get a kick out of this because she really hates this man for no reason, and yet for years he has continued to try to pet her. When we first met him a few years back, Sal and I were not yet married, and I would walk Gal by myself in the mornings and a couple of times we'd meet Ike. As soon as she heard those squeals coming from across the street, she'd go nuts. I'd look up to see why she was getting all crazy, and there'd be Ike walking across the street, chanting, "Gal-a-her, Gal-a-her, Gal-a-her." This guy just didn't get it, she *hated* him.

Four years into this, Sal and I were walking one Sunday morning, and I decided to go into a coffee shop to get us two iced coffees. As I came out of the shop, I saw Ike petting "Gal-a-her." He was explaining to my husband that there is a dog that looks just like "Gal-a-her" and that he had been trying to pet her for years but she was not friendly. Sal knew of Ike from my stories and put one plus one together. As I walked out of the shop I heard him saying to Ike, "Does the girl have brown hair, is tall and Irish looking?"

Ike replied, "Yes, yes, that's her. Do you know her?"

To which Sal responded, "That's my wife." At that moment, "Gal-a-her" realized that I was back out of the store and started growling at Ike. Sal and I still giggle when we think of Gallagher's motherly protection.

There are two other "Ike-types" in our area. The first is Louie. Louie is best likened to Klingher on M*A*S*H. He is close to seventy years old and sometimes wears ladies clothing, lavender and pink blouses, with boobs, and he loves gaudy dangling earrings. Despite being dirt poor, Louie has two dogs and four cats and proclaims himself an animal lover. Gallagher knows Louie is not 100% there and has forbidden him from petting her, Monster and Nuggie. He has tried for years to make friends with her, a couple of times compromising the integrity of his fingers. He just won't accept that Gallagher doesn't like him. How do I explain to him that she has discriminates against "the different?"

Then there's Billy. He is also "different" and can be found walking up and down the street babbling to himself. He is harmless, but his behavior upsets Gallagher. Billy loves dogs but seems to understand that Gallagher doesn't want to be his friend. He is the brightest of these three men. He understands that as soon as he approaches my house, if Gallagher is outside, even if she is in a deep sleep and he is not babbling, she still knows he is coming. She gets up quickly and gives him a big old Brooklyn attitude. She is amazing. After about ten attempts at making friends with her he has realized that she means business and now crosses the street instead of walking past my home.

Gallagher saves the day—Mow-Mow is discovered

Gallagher is more than just a big old mixed breed momma. She is a huge lover of kittens and cats. She can sniff out a kitty anywhere. In the ice cold winter of 1997, I was too lazy to walk her before going to work one morning and put her in the yard to do her business. As I stood in the doorway freezing, I kept calling her to come back inside. She wouldn't. She was too busy looking at a lean-to that we had built for a stray bunny that lived in our yard.

Yes, a stray bunny in Brooklyn, and whose yard did he choose to live in, despite the extremely dense population of Brooklyn? Mine, of course. Mr. Bunny had been with me for eighteen months and listened better than my dog! As soon as I would come out and call his name he would come running for his food. Mr. Bunny would eat the tops off of all my tulips and carrots out of my hand. My Dad fell in love with Mr. Bunny also and would come to visit him while I was at work, bringing him the peelings from carrots and potatoes. Mr. Bunny was so well fed, he had developed jowls.

Gallagher and Mr. Bunny had become best of friends, and she would always stand nose to nose with him, sniffing him. I think she thought he was the strangest looking and smelling cat she had ever seen! This one morning, Mr. Bunny had not come out for his breakfast and was nowhere to be found, but for some reason Gallagher would not come inside. She was obsessed with his lean-to, tilting her head sideways, trying to hear something. After a few minutes of calling her, I walked down the steps to the back of the yard to grab her collar to bring her inside. It was then that I realized that Mr. Bunny's lean-to was now the new home to a momma cat and her three babies. I had never seen this momma cat before and would never see Mr. Bunny again. I wonder what could have happened to him. If it weren't for Gallagher letting me know about these kittens, I would not have fed the momma and the kitties probably would have died! It was mid-March, the ground was frozen solid, and the garbage pickings were not very good. So I provided room-service for the new momma and tried desperately to make friends with the kitties as they got bigger. At this point in my life, I was still just a dog person, but knew that I had to help out this momma cat and her kittens. It was just too cold not to!

As winter turned to spring, the kitties turned from little mice like figures to kitties. They were adorable. Still the thought to find them a home never entered my mind. I just didn't have the whole animal rescue thing in me yet. I did continue to feed them but, like so many people, I didn't have any inclination to take the next step, finding them homes or getting them socialized and neutered. By May, the mother had disappeared completely. Still I fed the kittens. Then one day, two of the three were gone, never to be seen again. There must have been a big black hole that those animals disappeared into. They were gone, just like that. The only one left, I had nick-named Mow-Mow, because as soon as I came out and called her, she'd come running from wherever she was, meowing all the way. She always had a terrific appetite. One day this big, bad Tom Cat showed up and started harassing my Mow-Mow. How dare him! Mow-Mow was not fixed and barely four months old. So, I did what every outraged woman would do. I filled a water gun with vinegar and water, and every time he would try to have his way with my little friend, he would get doused! I think that over time he became immune to the smell, either that or just liked the challenge of trying to get her! Finally, in September, I decided to get Mow-Mow fixed. I took her to the vet, had it done, and released her back into the yard. She had become a real sweet cat, but still I had no desire to take her in. I was a dog person!

Each day, twice a day, like clockwork, I would feed her. She let me pick her up and often rubbed against my ankles when I came outside. I looked forward to seeing her, and if she missed a meal I worried. Late in September, she disappeared. For one full month, I did not see her. I was so worried about her. I thought she must have been stuck in a garage or something. We checked all the neighbor's garages by walking past them calling her name. She would surely respond to her name if she was there—she had a very loud meow. I was certain that if she were around, we'd find her. No luck. But each morning I'd go out and check and was disappointed each time. Then exactly one month after she disappeared,

I was sitting in my kitchen paying bills and out of the corner of my eye I saw a cat walking across the garage roof. I ran to the back door and called her name, and there she was, my Mow-Mow. She looked wonderful, not like she had missed any meals! I was so happy to see her. Still, I had no inclination to bring her inside, I was a dog person!

In December of 1997, the weather was awful, and I felt badly for Mow-Mow being out there in the frigid temps! Finally, I gave in. But it was only going to be until the spring. Once the weather was warm, she was *out*. But all these years later, she is still *in*, and I am crazy about her. She is an enormous, gentle, lazy cat, weighing at least twenty pounds. I tell her she's my big lump of butter. She is the first cat I had ever taken in and quickly has become one of a bunch. She owes her life to Gallagher. If Gallagher hadn't discovered her and her momma that day, I would never have fed the momma. If I hadn't fed the momma, she would've had to go away to search for food. Surely these kitties would have frozen to death without the warmth of their momma on those brutal March days!

Becoming an Animal Convesion Group, aka Rescue Group

It was the fall of 2004, and I had been looking to get involved in working with animals but couldn't get myself to go to the shelter. I found the whole shelter environment to be overwhelming, depressing and just too difficult for me to handle. Desperately though I wanted to help. So, I decided to start hosting adoption events. The idea was to bring the shelter pets to the neighborhood. Our area of Brooklyn did not have a single shelter or facility nearby where area residents could go to adopt a pet. As things were, the only way for people to get pets with ease was for them to reach deep into their pockets and purchase a pet from one of the handful of pet shops in the area. I believe that most people, given the choice, would rather adopt a pet and know they are saving a life, than buy a pet shop puppy.

Our first event went so well that we felt that we had to continue our efforts, so we planned another one for the following month. The animals are saved both at these events and during the time between events. One of my best friends, Joanne, works for a very busy vet in Bensonhurst, and we have developed a wonderful referral relationship. She refers to me three or four people a week who need help re-homing their pets for one reason or another. At the time of this writing, our Brooklyn community has saved over six hundred animals from euthanasia in a little over a year and a half.

In order to prepare for our first adoption event, I needed to put a carefully thought-out plan in place. Where would it be, who would help me, how to promote it and—the two most important details of all—where would we get the pets, and how would they be transported? Surprisingly, all of these things fell easily into place. I was amazed at how receptive people were. Although, there were still others who seemed to believe that no one would come to our event and that perhaps we shouldn't do it because we might end up disappointed. Being a tough Irish Brooklyn girl, I am not easily discouraged, and that worked to my advantage, especially in this case.

At the time I was working for another realty company and was lucky enough to have a very easy going boss. I approached him about the idea of hosting our first event there in the office. He was in complete agreement and even thought that it would be fun. The next thing on the agenda was to get someone to work closely with me on this project. I had become friends with Pat while working in that office. She was also an enormous animal lover. I decided that I would ask her if she would like to help me plan this event. Pat was taken with the idea. For the next year, Pat was 100% behind me in what soon became the most successful "animal conversion" effort to ever be implemented in our community.

Pat and I had three weeks to plan our first event. We worked like sled dogs, taking countless hours from our workweek to make sure that we planned a flawless day. We took out a front page advertisement in a local *Marketeer* magazine—with a circulation of 20,000. It cost us $1,000 out of our pockets. We had a local newspaper run a little article letting people know that there would be an "adoption event" taking place in the neighborhood. We had my talented twelve year old nephew Johnny make us the funniest, coolest fliers on his computer to help promote the event. We made thousands of copies and plastered them everywhere in the community and all of the surrounding areas. It took us days in the freezing cold. We included our cell phone numbers on the fliers—who would have ever thought that we would get such a response? Our phone bills that month went through the roof! The excitement that was generated in anticipation of the big day was almost beyond description.

As the date approached, my sister Monica drove around with me and helped post fliers in the mornings. In the evenings, I'd recruit my husband for flier detail. Soon, my mom was asking for some to put up in the neighborhood. Getting the word out became a family affair, which would soon change into a community affair.

NOVEMBER 13, 2004

Our Very First Adoption Event

THE DAY BEFORE the event we had a Nor'easter! Crazy amounts of rain and fierce wind whipped through the neighborhood. Pat and I had a million last minute things to do and ended up soaked to the bone numerous times. We were grateful that this was all occurring on Friday and not Saturday—soggy dogs are not hot ticket items. We want them to look, smell and show their very best! Luckily, the morning of the event was a cold, crisp, crystal clear one! We met at 7:00 a.m. in order to make sure we had the coffee, bagels and refreshments set up. We blew up balloons to put outside to draw attention to our office and set up a registration table inside. We were ready for anything!

Amazingly, we had a woman show up at 7:30 a.m. with a baby in a carriage. She was there to adopt! She had taken three buses from her neighborhood to get to us and was determined to adopt a Husky she had seen the previous day at the shelter. The shelter would not release the pup to her because it was one of the five, yes five, dogs earmarked for our event. At the shelter the day before, she and another woman were fighting over this dog—but we had no idea about any of this. All we knew is that a woman had called us the day before from the shelter asking us for all the information about when we started and what time she could show up, to which we said 10:00 a.m. She said she was driving to us from Westchester to adopt a dog she had seen in the shelter but that they would not release to her because it was earmarked for our day. It turned out this dog was the same dog that the other woman wanted. Lo and behold, to begin our day we had quite the showdown between these women! When the bus arrived, they both wanted this beautiful pup! The poor pup had just been fixed the day before and was not interested in anyone or thing! She was in pain, plain and simple, and could care less about anyone in the room. She was miserable! The girls eventually worked it out and ended up leaving together! We were surprised and relieved. We had overcome our first hurdle of the day, but it would not end there.

As the event was approaching, it had become evident to us that we were going to be swamped with prospective adopters. We made sure that we communicated this to a woman we will call Anna, our liaison from the Animal Care and Control of NYC. Because of the sheer volume of phone calls we were receiving, Pat and I were confident that we could place at least 30 dogs and cats that day. Anna sent us five dogs, two of which were not adoptable for ACC policy reasons. Why send them? Well, I did ask . . . and was told that she would take all of her animals and leave if I was unhappy with her. I was angrier than I had ever been. Picture this . . . We had over 100 people sitting inside our office waiting for dogs and cats and countless people outside, patiently waiting on the cold windy, but luckily sunny sidewalk—and this is what she shows up with. This was the first and only negative experience I had with the ACC. Luckily, it all worked out in the end, and we went on to develop an invaluable relationship with these wonderful folks who work so hard to help save these deserving pets, but in the beginning things didn't look so swell.

A worker from The North Shore Animal League was on-board the bus that transported the pets. She heard my exchange with Anna and came to the rescue. Her name was Claire. I will never forget her or what she did that day! What a woman! Claire saw the turnout we had, immediately got on her cell phone, contacted her boss who was off that day, and made sure that we got more animals delivered to us! But, there was one problem—it was going to take two hours to get them to us! Amazingly, the crowd waited. After more than two hours the bus pulled up, loaded with pups and kitties. The scene on the street was chaos! People were cheering. I still get goose-bumps when I think of that moment. Everyone was thrilled. Twenty-eight animals were adopted that day! Twenty-eight! Not a bad number when I consider the way things could have gone if Anna had things her way!

At each event, there is always a person or pet or both that stand out for whatever reason. At this event that person was a senior citizen with gray hair in a bun who walked with a cane, named Ruth. Ruth showed up at the very beginning of our day and instantly bonded with a Mini-Pinscher that was just terrified about being exposed to so many people and noises. Instantly, she was crazy about this little fellow, and he was crazy about her. Ruth had a very calm, soothing voice and this went over beautifully with the little guy. She immediately wanted to adopt him, however, the dog could not be released from the shelter because he had been a stray and he hadn't been there forty-eight hours yet. However, he would be eligible for adoption the next morning!

Ruth was crushed and began to cry. She then tried to reason with Anna, but without any luck. Ruth figured that if the dog could not be released at that very moment, but could be released the next day, then she would pay the fee, complete the paperwork and first thing the next morning, she would take a car service to the other side of Brooklyn where the shelter was located and pick up the dog. Imagine being willing to do this for a little dog she just met! For policy reasons, Anna had to deny Ruth this possibility, and Ruth was inconsolable because of it. At that moment, Pat and I made a promise to Ruth to work with her on finding her something else, comparable to that dog, as soon as we could. A promise we were able to fulfill at the February event.

With the insanity of the day being as it was, Pat and I never had a moment to eat, not even a bagel in the morning. We were starving and running on only adrenaline by the end of the day. Once the animals were gone, we immediately began the cleanup, which was a huge undertaking. However, we were lucky enough to have a few kind people from the office stay around and help us. Pat and I did not realize just how wrecked we were until all the work was done. Once we had the opportunity to sit and reflect on our day, it was at that moment that we realized that we were starving and most importantly, we were onto something spectacular. What a raging success our day was—exhausting but wildly successful! What more could we ask for? We met wonderful people that day. We developed new friendships, and we also got a following of pet loving people who are now steady volunteers with us! Results—we got 'em! We were on top of the world.

My first order of business on Monday morning was to see to it that I communicated to Anna's boss how unhappy I was with what had transpired. Throughout the day on Saturday, I had overheard little arguments at the adoptions table where she was sitting. The snip-its that I was able to hear further strengthened my case. It wasn't just me she had the problem with, it was everyone! I had so many people come up and ask who the "witch" at the table was. I decided that it would be in her boss's best interest, as well as the animals' best interest, that he be fully informed of her actions and attitude at Saturday's event.

I made a point of finding out to whom she reported and sat down and proceeded to write a letter. Believe me, it was a letter that no one would have wanted written about them! I was angry and to the point. I wanted to make sure that this woman never had the opportunity to do this again to me or any other person willing to volunteer to host a day like ours. While I typed away busily on the computer with no shortage of adjectives to describe Anna, I received a call from a woman from North Shore Animal League, Joanne. Joanne is Claire's boss, the lady who saved the day on Saturday! I was thrilled to speak with her. I made sure that she understood just how critical Claire's actions were to the success of our day. I sang Claire's praises to her for the next few minutes. Then, she paid us high compliments and tried to mend fences between us and the ACC. She had Ed Boks call me. At the time he was the head of the ACC. Ed apologized for Anna's actions and asked to hear my version of the events.

The results—twenty-eight pets adopted out in one day—spoke volumes. Ed, being an intelligent guy, realized that I was not a relationship he wanted to lose. I was a valuable resource and with my background, willingness to help and enthusiasm, would prove to be someone he not just wanted, but needed, to continue to have work with their organization. Ed got an earful from me. From what we understand, most of the smaller events that are conducted off-site yield five to ten adoptions; twenty-eight was truly an accomplishment. I explained to Ed that I was more than confident that I could replicate these results with great ease, but with one stipulation—that Anna never pop her miserable little head into my space or my event ever again. I never dealt with her after that, and my experiences with everyone else from the ACC have been nothing short of spectacular.

Of the twenty-eight animals adopted that first day, I see four of them around the neighborhood frequently. I refer to them as my "God-children." I enjoy running into them on their walks or in the park. Many times the owners will bring them by my real estate office to visit and to share their wonderful stories with me. I can't begin to say how good this makes me feel.

One of them is named Willie. Willie lives three blocks from my home and, as life would have it, ended up living in a home that belonged to an old woman who had recently passed away. This woman's name was Beuhla. Beuhla was the biggest dog lover alive. I had befriended her about five years before she passed away, while out walking my dog. She had the most handsome yellow Lab named Buddy. Bud was what I still refer to as a perfect specimen. When Beuhla passed away, the house was sold. Lucky for Bud, one of the wonderful neighbors took him in to live with her family. Anytime I walk by and see Willie sitting on Beuhla's porch, I think to myself that she is up in heaven smiling at this terrific pup enjoying her porch—a porch that she made a point of telling me how much she loved sitting on, watching the world go by with "her boy, Bud."

Willie was one of the very last dogs to be adopted that day. He was sitting in the window of the real estate office, and no one was even looking at him. Why would they? He was about five months old, kind of big and ordinary looking. His competition was fierce—the rest of the animals around were cute, pot-bellied pups, with puppy breath. Willie just sat there, so dejected looking.

Because of the vast number of people that had been crammed into our small office, I had not even seen him until a very shy, unassuming young man came up to me and asked if Willie was still available. I went to see which pup he was talking about, and it was then that I met this loveable dog. Sure he was available, I excitedly told him. I asked him what drew him to this pup, and he said it was because the pup looked sad and that he had been watching and not even one person looked at him. I instantly knew that this was a truly compassionate person, one that I would feel really good about adopting this pup. I took Willie out of the window and held onto him until his new owner processed the paperwork, which took about a half hour. What a special, timid little boy this pup was. I was so happy that Willie was getting a home. As Willie and his new daddy walked out the door, I could not figure out who was more excited, father or son.

Another adoptee from that day was Shorty. Shorty was a white Corgi mix. He was so silly looking that he was cute. Shorty was about three years old and part of the original five that came to the event that morning. When he first arrived, he was just so happy to get out of the van! He didn't know what to do first, so he relieved himself on the magazine rack belonging to the real estate office. Good Boy! Within an hour, he was adopted by a lovely Spanish family who were completely crazy about him.

The third one that I see around is Rocky. Rocky's new home is literally a stone's throw from my new office. Rocky was also part of the original five. He was a purebred black and white Pointer. Rocky was a very nervous soul. I could see that he was overwhelmed by the experience of being transported from the shelter to our office. Goodness knows where he came from, but at about five years old, he was not all that thrilled about not having an owner. I do believe that animals have expressions on their face, and his expression that day was one of desperation. He desperately needed someone to love him. Luckily, a nice forty-ish single guy came along and adopted him! Pat and I were so thrilled to see Rocky getting a home. Once the paperwork for the adoption was completed, Rocky seemed to get a look of relief on his face and proudly strolled off down Fifth Avenue with his new daddy. It was not until a week later that I found out that this man who had adopted Rocky was once a shy little boy named Thomas that I had gone to school with and had not seen since 1977! What a small world.

Rocky is still a shy, nervous guy, but his owner is wonderful about dealing with his issues and makes sure that Rocky always feels safe, secure and loved!

The fourth one I see is a beautiful male orange kitty. He was a peanut when he was adopted by a fellow realtor named Rita. She instantly fell in love with him and named him Rocky. This was the second Rocky of the day! Kind of funny because the real estate office I was working for was a Prudential Office and the rock is the logo . . . Rocky has grown up quickly into a feisty, fun-loving kitty, spoiled beyond words. Rita is thrilled to death to have him because when she adopted him; she was still mourning the loss of her cat who had recently passed on and her life was missing that special something that we as pet owners know all too well . . . the magic that a pet provides.

During the weeks after our adoption event, our phones continued to ring. People from all over Brooklyn were calling us because they missed the event and wanted a pet, or because they had a dog or cat that they couldn't keep and needed a home, or because they had found a pet that needed us to help it!

It was as these calls began to accumulate that we realized we needed to start keeping lists: lists of the names of people who called, when and why. As time went on we began to make love connections between the callers. The effect kept snowballing. Within no time, we were placing a few pets a week. Then the rescues began. People would start calling us about pets in need, and Pat and I would drop everything we were doing and go out on our missions. Pat is a wonderful, patient friend that I am lucky to have. She and I have done many rescues together, all over the Brooklyn and Staten Island. She never says no! The only problem with doing what we are doing is that it gets to be very pricey. I have spent thousands of dollars out of my own pocket on vet bills since beginning this "crusade." Very few people offer to help, even if you are going out of your way to help them with their pet situation. How can you just expect someone to come to your rescue, spend a fortune out of their own pocket to assist this animal that you called them about and then not even reach into your pocket to provide a little token of appreciation or compensation? Do they think that the vets I go to are *free?* I don't say anything because I would never allow money to come between me and my helping a pet. It's not about the money anyway.

DECEMBER 12, 2004

The Second Adoption Event

WE STILL HADN'T come up with the idea of naming the events because we hadn't yet realized what a huge success they were going to continue to be. But based on the number of phone calls we were getting from people who wanted to know when our next event was, we decided to host another one, just four weeks after the first! It was December 12, 2004, a very gray day. This event was held at our real estate office's mortgage company. The space was bigger, and we were even more organized this time. We had a huge poster created by a professional printer made for the storefront window reading, "On December 12, this place is going to the dogs!" with all the rest of the details of our day. We also spent another $1,000 on advertising, countless hours in the bitter wind posting fliers all over Brooklyn and more countless hours responding to phone calls. The local newspaper ran a terrific article praising us and promoting our next event. This adoption stuff could easily become a full-time job in no time, but a full-time job that we really love and can't get enough of! We were really enjoying ourselves!

The morning of the event, we decorated the place with animal things, purchased coffee, bagels, cookies and candy. What a spread we provided! We had tablecloths, gift bags, raffles and all kinds of wonderful things set up for the crowds. The day was to begin at 11:00 a.m. Believe it or not, word had spread so much about us and the success of the last event that people began showing up—in the cold—at 9:30 a.m.!

By the time the bus from North Shore pulled up filled with pets from the ACC, we had wall to wall people, literally a long line of people waiting to board the bus! It was chaos once again, but good chaos. This overwhelming response from the community was tear-jerking! All these people, waiting in the freezing cold to help adopt a pet that faced death if sent back—how cool was this? What a wonderful bunch of folks! The line for the bus was so long that I was forced to keep order by using the sign in sheets that we had prepared. One by one I called the names. On the bus was a litter of eight pups. They were said to be a Border Collie/Lab mix. They were eight weeks old and had the whole puppy belly and puppy breath thing happening. I am such a sucker for that! Anyway, they looked so much like my Buckwheat when he was a puppy that it brought back bittersweet memories for me. It felt like yesterday that I had gotten my Buckwheat as a Christmas present at the very same age. The time with him went too fast! In the blink of an eye it seemed to be over.

As the people boarded the bus everyone fell in love with the puppies. Some were solid black and some were black and white. I could see from the paws that they were going to be big, but others on the bus said, "No, forty pounds." I knew that they'd be forty pounds when they were five months old, but I didn't want to get into an argument with the "experts," so I let it go. There were some people adopting the pups that I didn't think were a good fit, but because they were signed in early we were forced to allow them to adopt. This upset me because there were far more suitable people at the end of the line who missed the chance to adopt one of these guys.

I was lucky enough to know three of the people who adopted the pups. The first was a couple I knew because of their dog, Kansas. Kansas had died recently, and they were heartbroken over it. Ann and Bob had no children. Because of that, they had the luxury of really doting on their pets; this was the kind of owner I craved for these pets! They adopted a beautiful little boy, black and white and named him Dundee. Dundee turned out to be a devil. Within no time he weighed much more than the forty pounds the "experts" had predicted, and a year later he was still growing and passing the seventy pounds mark.

Dundee's nickname is DundeeDoubleB. The DoubleB stands for Bad Boy. He is a big, silly beast! I call him my Godchild and love when they come by the office to visit, even if his tail does knock over everything it touches. Dundee is an extremely handsome dog with a beautiful tail. He is truly a happy fellow and lunges to say hello to anyone who even looks his way on the avenue. He is so full of love that it is exploding out of his body! Ann and Bob are crazy about him, even if Bob is stuck doing all the walking because Dundee turned out to be much more than the forty pounds of dog that Ann could have handled!

Another pup from that litter was adopted by an Irish family. I mistakenly believed that this was another wonderful home because, being Irish, I knew that Irish people were big animal lovers and were almost always very kind hearted souls. The couple was adopting the dog for their ten year old daughter as a Christmas gift. They were so excited about it, and I was just as excited for them and for the dog. They named him Bunny, and all seemed to be going well. Bob, Dundee's owner, would stop into the bar they owned to compare notes on their pups and would always share the information with me. I loved to hear the progress reports, even if Bob complained about how well behaved Bunny was according to his owner and that he got a brat. Whenever Bob complained to me about Dundee I always said, "So, do you want a refund?" Unfortunately, the lovely Irish family overestimated how smart and how well trained their lovely pup was and on a Sunday afternoon took him to a local park that was not fenced in and that had extremely high volumes of traffic running on all sides of it. They let the dog off the leash. Within moments, the dog saw a squirrel, chased it into the street and was killed instantly. When Bob stopped me to tell me the sad news, I didn't know if I was more angry or sad. No fence around the yard, young super-energetic pup, lots of squirrels—a recipe for disaster.

The third pooch was adopted by friends of my sister. Their black Lab had recently died, and they wanted something just like him. The couple also had a ten year old daughter who was with them and helped to pick the dog out. Since they had big dogs before and the dogs always lived long lives, I had no big concerns. I never got much information on the dog they named Ralph, but from the little I did hear, it sounded like Ralph was deserving of the DoubleB middle name as well. He liked to eat rocks and was extremely strong willed and very difficult to house-train. It didn't seem like they were enjoying him very much but wouldn't give him away no matter how frustrated they were with him. They'd deal with it. When anyone has a dog growing at the rate that these guys were, the last thing they want to have any trouble with is housetraining. I chuckled when I rehashed the adoption day in my mind; I had tried to sell these guys on a beautiful, housebroken, four year old beagle, but no, they wanted the pup.

We had a wonderful dog named Blue at the event that day. Blue had one blue eye and one brown eye. He was a big boy, at least eighty pounds and had the sweetest face. Because he wasn't a cute pup but rather a big mellow fellow, no one was really interested in him. Personally, he was my kind of dog: on the mellow side, mushy and sweet. As the day wore on he seemed to know that he was getting passed over time and time again and looked a little sad. Finally, this wonderful woman named Jeanette showed up. She fell in love with Blue, and he instantly perked up! She walked him inside, filled out all the paperwork and took off his adopt me vest, and they started their journey home! Goose-bumps! I had them all over. Sal and I were thrilled because we felt such a connection to this dog, and we knew there was no way we could take him home but by the same token knew if he went back he would be part of that awful statistic of the kill shelters.

Jeanette keeps in touch with me and has even brought Blue by one of our events to say hello. He looks wonderful, has gotten even bigger thanks to all of the good lovin' he's getting from her. She is crazy about him. They are a match made in heaven! Blue deserved to get a wonderful home because he was an easy dog to adopt, had no issues and would be pure pleasure! I was glad that Jeanette was able to see the beauty that he possessed, and she felt luckier than Blue to have him in her world!

As the day wore on, it became apparent that two of our dogs would not being going "home." We were so sad. One was an oversized black dog that was super strong! My 220-pound husband had walked him around the block and found him to be a challenge. His name was Magnum, and he was magnificent. But to most Brooklyn people with either small apartments or 20'x100' sized properties, he was a giraffe, a gentle one, but a still giraffe. He was heartbroken when put back on the bus that day, and so were we.

The other dog sent back got a raw deal. We had an emotionally disturbed older woman come in at the very beginning of the day, insisting on a small dog. We should have realized that she was a problem when she urinated all over the cloth chair in the office—but that is a completely different story. Patches was a small dog. Despite not being an ideal home, because she was first in line, she got first choice. I don't believe that first in line necessarily means the best home, and since this fiasco, I am now very vocal about it. This woman took over one hour at the adoption processing table, tied up the people there from helping anyone else, then took the dog. She kept it in her car for about an hour and then decided it was too active for her, so she pulled up in four lanes of traffic and came to a dead stop without pulling over and demanded that we "take this dog" and "give me that dog" as she pointed to a very large, but older dog. At this point, things began to get ugly; we didn't want her to have any dog and had to threaten her with calling the police in order to get her to leave. Sad but true! We had to do what was right for the animals.

Unfortunately, by this point many people looking for a small dog had left because there were none. This woman denied this poor little guy his chance at a good Brooklyn home. However, because of an act of kindness on the part of North Shore Animal League, they took this special dog back to their facility with them and Patches got his chance at a getting a home. We later heard that he did get adopted and that Magnum got adopted on Christmas Eve . . . Merry Christmas!

The one true kick-in-the-butt we got on that cold December day was the NYPD traffic department's need to ticket our people and the North Shore buses because of expired meters. Even though the local precinct had provided us with No Parking Signs for us to use to reserve these spots for ourselves and the bus, these power hungry uniforms decided that they would ticket us! We couldn't believe our eyes. I am not usually a name caller, and don't believe in being mean to anyone, but what kind of law enforcement was this? My volunteers and the bus were being ticketed! Here we were, legitimately helping the City of New York empty out their overcrowded shelters without killing pets and these officers were flexing what little muscle they had. Initially, we tried to reason with them, but they just ignored us! This caused all-Brooklyn to break loose—that's even worse than all Hell breaking loose, believe me.

The grand total of animals adopted out on that cold day was a tie with the first! Twenty-eight! What a terrific number! We were on fire! We were in the newspaper again, and we were becoming so well known in the area that people from all over were calling to talk to us about their pet "issues." We continued to make love connections between adoption events and started to find ourselves being termed a "rescue group."

As Christmas quickly approached, we decided that our events would start having themes. Since we agreed to host our next event on February 12, 2005, it would have a Valentine's Day theme . . . thus the "Lovey Dovey Adoption Event" was born. The name was compliments of my nephew John who had by this point become our official flier designer. He is the wittiest, brightest and most creative soul I have ever met. At twelve years old, he was just as good as any professional! He liked to refer to himself as John Inc., so, on the Lovey Dovey fliers he began to add, in very small letters, designed by John Inc. It made him giddy to see his fliers all over the neighborhood.

I, on the other hand, had become a current events project. My nephew Kevin, who was eight at the time, had to prepare a current events story for school, and unbeknownst to me, he chose to do his story about the adoption days, using the articles from the local paper. Around this same time my neighbor Carole, another animal lover who I have suckered into taking three pets from me over the years, tells me that her daughter Casey used me for her current events story for school. These kids were learning from me that a small, grassroots effort could really make a difference in this world, and I was really glad to be the one to teach them this lesson!

LIZA, THE VET TECH, TO THE RESCUE

Cindy Cat

J ANUARY 2005 WAS very snowy here in Brooklyn. We had a blizzard in mid-January and the outdoors was no place to live! I got a call from a woman named Delores. Delores was in her seventies and lived in the 1st floor rear apartment of a six family house in Bensonhurst. She told me she needed help with a kitten she'd rescued. Apparently Delores, like many other seniors in the neighborhood, feeds colonies of strays. During the blizzard she noticed that two of the kittens belonging to the colony were not doing so well. They were stuck in a snow bank and didn't seem to have the energy to get out of it. They were freezing to death. Delores went outside and brought them in. One died in her arms, which broke her heart; the other, once warmed up, jumped out of her arms and hid under her bed. She couldn't get the kitty to come out. Finally, after two days, she decided to crack open her window a bit and within the blink of an eye, the kitten jumped out from under the bed and wedged itself between the screen of the window and the glass. Delores panicked and called me to come and save it.

Once again, Pat and I went racing up to Bensonhurst to take a look at what was going on. It turns out that the kitty had attached itself to the screen with her claws and was adamant about staying put! Luckily, Delores was able to lend me some thick gloves. Also, the windows were the newer kind that tilted in for easy cleaning. So, with gloved hands, I grabbed the kitty as Pat tilted the window open. This three-to-four-month-old kitten was feral and terrified of people. She was hissing and spitting and trying to swat like crazy, but what a beauty she was. She had the most unusual coloring: a charcoal grey background with auburn, cream and brown mixed through. Pat and I quickly put her into a carrying bag and took her to my house. While in the carrier, I noticed she smelled awful. I couldn't figure out why, but would later on . . .

Once we left, Delores almost completely washed her hands of the kitty and didn't offer one penny for her care. When I got the kitty home I called her Cindy Cat. She just looked like a girl, pretty, very pretty. But Cindy was a very sick cat. My vet was closed for the day and was closed the next day too, so I waited about forty-eight hours to take her. She was eating, but she smelled so bad! I couldn't touch her or get near her to see what was wrong. When I wanted to open the cage, I had to put on a thick, long-sleeved sweatshirt and two pair of gloves just to feed her or clean the litter. This cat was scary—small but scary. She looked like she had feces stuck to her legs and her tiny little rear end, and I thought that was causing the smell, but I didn't dare try to clean her. She was just too wild and with so many other animals in my house, I was afraid I would just upset her even more by exposing her to them. As it was, I was keeping her in our hallway, where none of the other animals would see her.

When I took her to the vet, I left her there so that they could take a good look at her and keep her for what was supposed to be an overnight stay. Later in the day I got a call from Liza, the vet tech with the biggest heart in all of Brooklyn. She said that I had one very sick kitty on my hands. She had ear, eye and respiratory infections. She also had so much diarrhea stuck to her that the skin was actually all broken down and almost rotting away. This kitten was in terrible pain and discomfort! I felt awful and thought to myself that I would be just as grouchy as she was if I were in her shoes. Liza asked if she could hold onto Cindy for a week so that she could give her wound care three times a day. I was only too happy to have Liza handle her. I felt so sorry for the poor thing. As time went on, it turned out that Cindy had developed a problem in her rectum from having diarrhea so much as a baby. The condition would require laxatives and enemas for her whole life or they could try surgery, but there was no guarantee that it would be successful, as a matter of fact, she might always have a leaky butt if the surgery was not successful. I would be facing quite a vet bill but an even bigger dilemma! What to do? During this time I received a call from Delores asking how the cat was doing. I explained what was going on and that she was requiring lots of money and care. Delores acted shocked that a vet would charge us for this. Was she really this stupid or just putting on a fine act? Still, she did not offer a penny!

I didn't want to euthanize her, but then again, this kitty was feral and who would adopt a feral kitty that needed frequent enemas and laxatives? I was stressing about this big time. Finally, Liza asked me to let her keep her a while longer so she could work with her. She said that she had seen this once before and they were able to skip the surgery and work out a good protocol with the laxatives. If Liza was willing to work with me on this and give Cindy Cat a chance, then I was only too happy to accept her generous offer! So, Liza kept the kitty for four months, and I would check in weekly on her to get the progress report. Amazingly, Liza and her terrific staff were able to get Cindy socialized! And what is even more amazing, Liza got a friend, also a vet tech, to adopt Cindy Cat! Talk about a miracle! When it came time to settle the bill, Liza had capped the bill at $400.00 and that was all that I paid for all those months of wonderful care, all the meds, food, boarding and the dirty and difficult work of performing enemas on this sick little kitty! Few other vets would have shown this kind of compassion or kindness to a feral cat, of this I am sure! Liza is someone who would be the first person I visit if I were to win the lottery. Unlike many other vets, she is not quick to give up on a stray in need.

Tiffany

The winter of 2005 continued taking a toll on the outdoor cats. As we were walking the dogs one cold February morning, our friend Nora stopped us to beg me to help with a very sick cat. It was supposed to snow that evening, and she was afraid that the cat would freeze to death. I took the dogs home and came back to help out. Nora lived in an apartment building not far from my home. She was an avid animal lover, but due to personal problems was not in a position to be hands on with helping them with anything other than food, a warm box to provide shelter, and kind, comforting words.

When I arrived at Nora's building, it was freezing cold and I could feel that the snow would start falling very soon. Nora led me to a box in the bushes. Inside the box was a skeleton with white fur and enormous, sunken-in blue eyes. Nora had named her Tiffany, and in her day, she had been a stunning cat, but now she was a shivering bundle of bones that was moments away from death. I felt like throwing up. I had tears running down my cheeks as I picked up the little cat and put her into the carrier for our trek to the vet. My favorite vet was closed because it was Sunday, so I had to go to a place I didn't like as much.

Off we went, Nora in the passenger seat with Tiffany in her lap in the carrier. Tiffany never stopped purring the entire time. She was enjoying having the heat in the car blow directly on her near frozen body! The poor thing had eyes that were so blue and perfect but relayed to us just how hard her life was. She made us want to hug her and cry for all that she had gone through. When we arrived at the vet, we waited for almost three hours before we were taken into an examination room. By this time, Nora and I were emotionally drained and ready to cry, again! The vet tech was a woman with no personality or love of animals. She should have been a bathroom attendant instead. She took the cat's temperature and weighed her. Tiffany, a long, full grown cat weighed in at a measly five pounds. I was sick! My cats at home were three and four times heavier. This poor little momma! What heartbreak to watch! She had thick green mucus coming from both sides of her mouth, it was like strings; still, she purred and desperately wanted to have her head rubbed!

Eventually the vet came into the room. She took one look at the cat and gave us a look, like why are you here with this thing? She then looked at Tiffany's mouth. Her gums were snow white. She was severely anemic—a bad sign! We were then given the grim news, she probably had Feline AIDS or Leukemia, and she was extremely sick. The vet suggested we put her down. I said no! Do the blood tests and we'll talk. We left Tiffany there with very heavy hearts. Nora was very upset. She wouldn't even entertain the idea of euthanizing the cat; I was a little more balanced. I wanted to hear what the tests showed, and then we could go on from there.

The next day the dreaded call came. The receptionist called me on my cell phone and blurted out the following, "Mary Jo, the cat has Feline AIDS, do you want us to euthanize her?" Just like that; euthanizing her was the only option they were offering me. This infuriated me. This kitty had so much love in her that she deserved a chance. In addition to having AIDS, she was severely anemic and had a terrible infection in her mouth because of cracked teeth and sores on her gums. She was going to require long term antibiotics and lots of love, and then, just maybe, we could try to find someone to take her in.

As soon as I got off the phone with the receptionist from the vet's office, I called the vet's office that I love and spoke to Liza. I explained everything to her, and she said to bring the cat in, that she would look her over and try to work with her to get her strong enough to go to a place for AIDS-infected kitties in Pennsylvania. Liza knew the woman who ran it and visited her every couple of months with kitties that needed to be cared for there. Liza was more than willing to help me out with this cat. I was thrilled. I drove up to the other vet's office, picked her up in the carrier and drove her to see Liza. While on our way, Tiffany never stopped purring. She kept rubbing her face against the carrier and I kept putting my fingers in to try to give her a little much-needed comfort. She was oozing puss from her mouth at this point and was just a terrible mess. Along the way, I stopped for a moment and picked up my husband. Sal placed Tiffany on his lap and listened to her purr. I encouraged him to pet her, and when he saw the puss oozing from her infected little mouth, he had tears in his eyes. This kitty had such a winning personality that we instantly had to fall in love with her. She deserved a chance, and with Liza's help, she would have that chance.

Upon arrival at Liza's office, Tiffany was weighed. She was down to three pounds! She had lost two pounds in just two days! I was even more heartbroken because this said to me that she was not fed while at the other vet. I called them to ask them what they fed her—dry food.

Can you imagine that? The cat had a mouth full of broken teeth, open sores that are oozing puss and they fed her dry food! What were they thinking?

Liza worked with Tiffany for months getting her mouth healed up and her iron levels up. Upon arrival her iron levels were dangerously low and within a few months Liza was able to get them to a normal level. The infection in her mouth was clearing up nicely and she was able to eat soft food with no trouble. Of course, Tiffany had succeeded in winning over the staff, they were crazy about her. Instead of being sent to Pennsylvania, Tiffany ended up being the 3rd floor resident kitty until she was as strong as a normal kitty. They called her Granny. Everyone loved her! She was in a warm, safe and loving environment surrounded by people who would monitor her to make sure that she stayed as healthy and happy as possible. After a few months of good health, Liza brought her home to her mom, and Tiffany lived for almost a full year before dying in January. But that was a year that she would never have had if it weren't for Liza and her true love of her profession and of animals. Yet another example of why I love Liza the vet tech. She is a truly wonderful person who is not in it for the money. For Tiffany, she froze the bill at $275! I cannot even begin to thank Liza for all the wonderful things she does for the countless hopeless pets that come her way!

Liza Saves the Day Again—Foxy

The news reports were warning of another Nor'easter heading our way. Geez, if we listened to what they said, we'd think the end of the world was coming! It was a gray Friday morning, and I was walking to the supermarket one block from my house. As I walked across the street, I saw two people fussing over something small and looking rather perplexed. Being a nosy person, I glanced as I passed by to see what they had. It was a pathetic Pomeranian. Immediately my doggie mommy gene kicked in, and I was all over it. The girl holding him was so upset. She was on her way to work and had just found the dog lying on her back in the gutter. The poor dog had such an enormously bloated belly that she was stuck on her back and wasn't capable of turning herself right side up. The fur was so long and matted she looked like she was wearing a Rastafarian wig! Her nails were so overgrown that they were eating into her paw pads! This dog was a really terrible case of abuse and neglect. Where she came from was anybody's guess. Clearly she'd been dumped; the dog could hardly walk and there was no way she'd run away!

The girl who found her was running late for work and reluctantly left the dog with me. I immediately took the poor little thing to my groomer and asked her to please see what she could do with her to make her comfortable—especially those terrible overgrown nails! I left her there, and we nicknamed her Momma. Two hours later I went back and picked her up. She looked like a different dog. All cleaned up she was a really cute little thing, and they put an adorable little green bandana on her.

I made an appointment to bring her to the vet and have her checked out. She was not the healthiest specimen. She had bad teeth, small lumps on her breasts and a mild heart murmur. Other than that, she was okay. I kept her overnight, and she had terrible diarrhea. I felt so sorry for the poor little thing. I didn't know if it was nerves, change in diet or a virus. I was very worried about her. We put her on flagyl, and she seemed to improve greatly. Next, I needed a home for her. Vanessa, a young girl from the vet's office, offered to take her. I was happy because I knew her and figured she would give Momma a good home. But, it turned out that her dog didn't like Momma, so she brought it to work and Liza took it! Once again, it was Liza to the rescue! Liza brought this dog home to her mom who was wheelchair bound. Liza's mom named her Foxy, after the Foxy lettuce dog. Foxy ended up having the most wonderful life. She was a lap dog in every sense of the word. Liza's mom was crazy about her and doted on her constantly. Foxy lived for about two years and then died of some kind of heart problem. I felt bad, but I know for sure that she had wonderful care and lots of love during the last few years of her life, and that was all we can hope for when placing an older dog—or any pet for that matter.

X, OUR POSSESSED CAT

LIKE I HAVE mentioned before, Sal's the cat guy. I was never a cat person, but somehow Sal managed to get me interested in them and got me over my fear of picking them up and playing with them. When I met Sal he had two cats, X and Kookie. X was short for Exorcist. Sal called her that because she sounded like she was possessed. X showed up as a stray one hot summer day, many years before. Sal felt sorry for her and began to feed her. He already had Kookie and wasn't looking for another pet. Problem was, X made herself irresistible. She was a pretty soft gray kitty with a soft peach colored belly. She was cute, young, funny and persistent. She wouldn't take no for an answer. Each day she worked her hardest to get Sal to see what a great little kitty she was.

Weeks went by and Sal continued to feed her. Then it began to rain. It rained for days, and poor X was out in it all the time. Sal felt so sorry for her that he decided to take her in, much to Kookie's dismay. Kookie was so upset by X's arrival, that she spent the next *year* under the couch. This broke Sal's heart! X was a very dominant cat. She seemed to be very tough, fresh and had plenty to say. She constantly made these insane noises and hissed for no reason at all. It turns out that she has no idea what hissing is. She just likes to hiss, but there's never anything mean following the hissing.

When Sal and I got married, X was already close to ten years old. She had never lived with dogs before so we were concerned that she would have a hard time adjusting. She surprised us. She could care less about them. She just continued being X, hissing as she walked along, kind of like a mentally ill person mumbling to themselves. That was enough to keep the dogs from expressing any interest in being close to her. In a relatively short period of time, we've brought in two more dogs, Monster and Nuggie and three more cats: Mow-Mow, Sofia and Machi. Amazingly, she adjusts with ease to any newcomer we bring in. She just makes it plain that she is beyond the "horseplay" years and the new-comers seem to respect that. It is really quite remarkable how she commands such respect, especially since she is a tiny cat—only about eight pounds, which by our standards is tiny.

X has attached herself to me. When I sleep X has to sleep on top of me. I am an extremely light sleeper and having her touching me and purring loudly keeps me awake. I repeatedly try to get her to cuddle up with Sal but she refuses to. I have lost many hours of sleep because of this purring machine, but what can I do? If a kitty loves you, you can't be mean to it and lock it in another room. So, the end result is that I walk around sleep deprived most of the time! Oh the price we pay for loving our pets!

FEBRUARY 2005

The Lovey Dovey Adoption Event

WE WERE ON fire by this point! Having two unbelievably success-ful events under our belt did wonders for our enthusiasm and confidence. We were more than sure that we could continue to duplicate these results! What could be better than the feeling of send-ing the bus back empty or with only one or two pets on it? Knowing that I and my volunteers are the reason that all of those anxious faces will be sleeping in a warm home that night rather than in a cold, steel cage in a loud and scary shelter is beyond priceless.

Picture it. A huge bus from North Shore Animal League over-flowing with barking dogs and meowing cats pulls up on a street in Brooklyn. The lines of people waiting to take home their future pets are stretching in many directions. Once again it's chaos, but chaos in a good way. Everyone shares the same enthusiasm about wanting to help save a pet from being sent back to die. The energy in the air is thick and exciting.

Since this was our third event, we felt like we were becoming pros. After each event, we reflected on what worked, what didn't and what we could have done better. By this time, we were on our way to throwing the best events imaginable. Because we were lucky enough to secure a local Episcopalian church for this event, we would have tons of space. The church was gorgeous. The church grounds had beautiful buildings and a lovely garden and parking lot. In Brooklyn there aren't too many churches that have as pretty a setting as this church. The indoor and outdoor space that was being made available to us was priceless. If the weather were to be less than good, we would have a space to bring the dogs indoors, and even more than that they were *welcomed!* Another wonderful thing was that all it cost was the money for the porter. The porter was a terrific guy named Todd, and he had an older dog named Sammy. Sammy was the coolest dog and loved the perks that came along with being on-site when we were setting up. Everyone doted on him, and he got plenty of treats as all the ladies gushed, "Oh Sammy, you're so handsome!" Todd was a huge pet lover and really believed in what we were doing, so he never got bent out of shape about water bowl spills or "accidents" that happened. That was what the mop and paper towels were for. He provided service with a smile.

As is the case before every event, we worked like dogs promoting this day. We put out our usual thousands of fliers in the freezing cold and most of the time trudging through big mounds of snow that had been shoved against the poles that we so desperately needed to post our fliers on. Many times we found ourselves with snow coming over the tops of our boots and soaking our ankles and feet. That didn't stop us. We were too determined to make sure that everyone knew about our event. For a bunch of reasons, this event was even more special than the previous ones. First and foremost, the space. We were so excited about using the church. Second, we had decided on a theme for this one, the "Lovey Dovey Adoption Event," so we had great fliers to post. Third, we were including in this event a Senior for Senior Adoption Day; this meant that there would be a wonderful selection of older pets for the senior citizens to adopt with the fee waived for the adoption! Fourth, we actually had a few people who were willing to volunteer to help us! This was a big deal. In the beginning we hadn't realized how much we needed the extra hands the day of the event, and it was wonderful to have so many people ready, willing and enthusiastic to help! And lastly we were decorating the grounds and parish house to compliment our Lovey Dovey theme!

Decorating was so much fun. The parish house of the church could be described as a nice gymnasium with a stage. It was equipped with many chairs and large tables for us to decorate with bright red and pink tablecloths. We purchased bright red doggie and kitty water bowls with little paw prints all around the edges and filled them with all kinds of candy and placed them on each table. We got pencils that were painted red with little white hearts on them and placed them on all the tables so that the potential adopters could fill out their applications. We had red and pink balloons both inside and outside. Two tables were set up with coffee and tea and all kinds of Brooklyn bagels—there is nothing like a Brooklyn bagel, ask anyone. We had all the good stuff to put on the bagels and plenty of muffins and cookies.

All around the walls we hung heart shaped decorations and posters filled with pictures from our previous events depicting the animals being taken home by their new owners. In addition, we had taken all of the newspaper articles that were published about us and made big posters of them so people could read about what we had accomplished already and what we hoped to accomplish in the future. By doing all of these things, we transformed a vanilla-cone type of room into a strawberry shortcake type of room, and all that hard work was reflected in the energy that was being generated by the crowd of people waiting for pets.

Before the bus pulled up, we literally had a few hundred people waiting. Everyone was anxious about seeing what we had to offer. We had countless people asking for "smalldogs." Everyone wanted a "smalldog." "Smalldog." The way they said it, like it was one word, like it was a new, special kind of a breed! It was to a point where I felt like snapping at anyone who asked me that question. What is such a big deal about "smalldogs?" I don't get it. I have two small dogs and one large dog. Knowing what I know about my small dogs, I would rather have big ones! Sure they're cute, but they can be very yippy, yappy and spiteful! Not to mention that the fufu ones can cost a fortune in grooming at the end of the year!

By the time the bus arrived, the parish house was filled to capacity with standing room only. You would have thought that we were giving away winning lottery tickets with the number of people we had that cold February morning. I have to admit, it was a great credit to Pat and

I to have generated such a turnout. It meant that we had done an excellent job at promoting the event. After all, it was just the two of us doing all the leg work, so even if they tanked we had to take the responsibility for that as well. We were almost giddy at the turnout. There was one small problem though. Everyone wanted to be *first*. People started showing their Brooklyn attitudes a bit, and that wasn't pretty. So, what to do? I did what any strong Brooklyn woman would do. I got up on a chair so that everyone in the room could see and hear me and made an announcement that went like this, "Thanks so much for coming out on this cold morning to our "Lovey Dovey Adoption Event!" We are thrilled to have you here. The turnout is a true credit to the Bay Ridge Community and speaks volumes about the number of pet lovers we have here! In the spirit of keeping this a nice, peaceful and happy event, I just want to make sure that everyone understands one thing. We will not tolerate anyone fighting over who was first! We understand that there are a lot of people here, and we hope that everyone finds what they are looking for. If you don't find what you wanted, please sign the poster that is hanging by the door. Fill in all the information and we will keep you in mind for the pets that we get in between events. Again, fighting will not be tolerated, and if you start a fight you will be asked to leave. Thanks, and have a terrific day!"

My little speech worked well and for the most part we had a very peaceful day. Because we had such a huge turnout, of course, many of the people left empty handed. Once again, we made a point of letting them know that we would be hosting many more of these events throughout the year and that we would certainly be happy to keep their names and what they were looking for, and that we would work hard to find them a pet before the other events, if we got anything that suited them.

As with every event, there were always a couple of dogs or cats that stand out in my memory. This day we had two. The first was a tiny little dog named Lili. Like I mentioned before, everyone wants a "smalldog," so when the bus pulled up and the doors opened, the search began from outside the bus. It took about ten minutes to unload all the dogs. We left the cats on the bus in the cages but any dog that was not a young puppy got to come off the bus and mingle with the crowd. As we disembarked the dogs, we put colored bandanas around their necks to make them look even more appealing. While we were doing this the crowd became slightly impatient but excited at the same time. It was a necessary step because if we were to leave the dogs on the bus, they would lose their minds. This time, as soon as I stepped onto the bus, I made eye contact with the most precious, delicate little dog. She was almost all white and though full grown, she was super small. What struck me even more than her delicate features was that she was shivering uncontrollably. Between being terrified and freezing cold, she was a mess. As I began to feel overwhelmed with pity for her, I realized that she was a Papillion. I had promised my good friend Ruth, the woman with the cane from the first adoption event, that I would find her a Papillion. I couldn't believe my eyes. God was giving me a sign that this was going to be a wonderful day!

I hadn't seen Ruth yet that morning but I wouldn't dream of letting this dog get away from her, so I took my life into my hands by taking the dog out of her cage and bringing her inside with me! The crowd went nuts! Everyone was yelling at me that they were there first and where was I taking the "smalldog?" Blah, Blah, Blah. I almost started a riot, but I didn't care. This dog had Ruth written all over it, and even if I had to fill out the adoption papers and pay the fee myself, I would do it to make certain that Ruth got what she deserved. For the three months since our first event, Ruth had come into our office religiously asking if we had a "smalldog" for her, but in the past month, she had specifically asked that we find her a Papillion. She'd had one in the past named Rusty and loved him so very much. Pat and I had promised her that we would find her one, and I was going to make sure that I kept my word.

I ran inside the parish house and grabbed my cell phone. Then I had to search through my notebook for Ruth's telephone number. My hands were shaking as I held onto this priceless little ball of white fur. Lili shook like crazy in my arms so I had her inside my sweatshirt to make her feel warm and secure. I found Ruth's number and quickly dialed. Her husband answered and said that Ruth was not home. My heart sank. I asked him when she'd be back and he said he didn't know and that she was out shopping. Things would get ugly if I had to have this "smalldog" hanging around all day while I waited to bring it to Ruth. So, as I started to explain to Ruth's husband who I was and why I was calling, he began to chuckle and tell me that Ruth was on the bus on her way down to our event. I ran outside to see if I could spot Ruth in the crowd. Sure enough as soon as I exited the parish house there was Ruth walking up the driveway. I screamed out her name and told her that I had her dog! She immediately lost twenty years off her step and almost ran up to me to see. Ruth began to cry with excitement. She was so thrilled. And so the love story of Ruth and Lili began. Ruth was the first adoption we processed that day. She wrapped Lili in her wool scarf and called a car service to take them home. What a terrific match.

I called Ruth the next day to see how things were going. It turned out that Lili was not completely housebroken and had done her business in the center of Ruth's kitchen table. Ruth thought this was hysterical. She thought everything this little dog did was hysterical. She said she'd just go buy lots of paper towels. What a terrific attitude and what a lucky dog! Ruth spent a fortune on the dog. She bought Lili a wardrobe of cute coats and sweaters and, of course she had matching leashes for each outfit. She bought her an Outward Hound Stroller in which Lili sits quite happily while Ruth strolls the avenue with her. Lili made a huge difference in Ruth's social life. Lili had given her a reason to go out and the opportunity to meet so many new people. Ruth's home, just as I imagined, turned out to be the most wonderful home we could have possibly placed little Miss Lili in.

And who can forget Harry? I held Harry for so many hours that my elbows felt like they were locked in a cradling position. Harry was a twelve year old purebred Shitzu. He was black and white and the most pathetic looking dust mop of a dog I had seen. Harry's paperwork said that he had been found wandering on the street and picked up as a stray. Blarney! Harry wasn't a runaway, he was a throw away! At these events, I found myself guessing what had happened to these pets, how they ended up on the street. My guess with Harry was that belonged to an elderly person who had passed away and the people responsible for emptying the home or apartment tossed him out like trash! Harry's nails were so overgrown that the little man couldn't walk properly. The poor guy looked like he had been neglected for a long time. His fur was long and all matted. He was missing teeth and his little mouth smelled awful. There was no way we were going to get him adopted out to anyone other than one of our volunteers. He was the saddest little pooch we had seen, so far. Because he couldn't walk, I carried him most of the day. He loved being held and petted. He was not at all snappy and was quickly becoming my little lover boy. I approached everyone who walked in the door. No takers. His appearance was working against him, and no one would even consider him once they found out how old he was. But it wasn't fair. He deserved to go home that day! He deserved to enjoy the last few years of his life in a nice, cozy place. Towards the end of the day I switched off with a couple who were volunteering. These two women already had three dogs and a cat of their own but also the biggest hearts of anyone I had ever met. By the end of the day, myself, this couple and another volunteer named Margaret, had all decided separately that we would adopt Harry. It was unbelievable that Harry had so many takers! In the end the couple took him home.

Initially, I was concerned that Harry would be overwhelmed with their crew of pets. I was thrilled to find out that after a good grooming and nail clipping Harry seemed years younger! He fit in perfectly with the other animals and was quite happy to have the company. Now Harry is always at the dog run and is loved by all the other dogs. He has quickly become a little celebrity in the neighborhood because he is such a lovable little dude. Another happy ending!

At the end of the day we sent back very few pets. As usual, it is never easy to send any back, but we don't have a choice. That is why we can't stress enough to people to adopt rather than purchase. Choose to save a life!

SPRING 2005

It's Raining Cats and Dogs Adoption Event

S O MUCH FOR using the word *rain* in our title, that won't happen again! It rained! For the very first time the weather didn't cooperate with us. It didn't pour all day, but it certainly did get the dogs wet and made for a smelly dog day.

Preparing for these events had become fun for us. This time we went out and bought very colorful tablecloths to decorate the parish house, and then we blew up very colorful balloons, so despite cloudy weather we had sunshine indoors. We also went above and beyond in supplying all of our guests with free coffee, tea, muffins, Brooklyn bagels and spreads and candy. We re-used our dog bowls from the previous event and once again filled them with candy for all the tables. We seemed to have so many things down to a science at this point that I no longer lost sleep the night before the event.

For me the weeks leading up to this event were hellish. I was opening my own real estate office the Tuesday before the event. It had been a very stressful couple of weeks. For many reasons, I tried to keep the news of my impending opening as quiet as I could, but in a tight-knit community like this, where everybody knew everybody's business, that proved to be a challenge. Since I would be opened for business before the event, I decided that it would be a nice touch to have all of my volunteers dressed in the same color t-shirts with my realty logo and address on the front and with the words "Adopt a Shelter Pet" in large letters on the back. I ordered eight dozen shirts. I dressed all of the volunteers in bright orange and gave out blue and green ones to the people who adopted. Also, I had decided that whatever color t-shirt the volunteers would be wearing, that would be the color of the bandanas that we put on the dogs. It looked great.

Our usual method of promoting the event was hitting a snag. We had always used our telephone number and names on our fliers in case anyone wanted more information or needed help with an animal. This practice had to come to an abrupt stop. Early one morning, about two weeks before the event, Pat got a call from a Dept. of Sanitation Supervisor. The reason for his call was to warn us that he was going to give us twenty-four hours to take down all of the fliers that we and our volunteers had posted on the poles. If we didn't take them down, he would be ticketing us on a per flier basis. Pat pointed out to this man that we were saving lives! What we were doing was important. As much as he said he agreed with the sentiment, he still insisted that we pull down our fliers and that we not post any in the future.

Initially we were really worried, but we were not going to let it extinguish our enthusiasm and desire to produce great results. The pets needed us and that was all that mattered. After much deliberation, Pat and I decided to stand our ground. We decided that we would not be bullied into taking our signs down and that if we did get ticketed we'd fight a good fight. How could a city that is euthanizing animals by the thousands argue with what we were trying to do? It just made no sense. We continued to post our fliers, except that we deleted our contact information and our names. It was unfortunate we had to do that, but at least the information about the event was still getting out there!

Despite the rain we still had a strong turnout. The downside was that we had a lot of large dogs and hardly any "smalldogs." The two smallish dogs we had turned out to have very unhappy endings. When we got too many big dogs or Pit Bulls, this scenario was disappointing for us only because so many people didn't want or couldn't have large dogs and that means having to send them back. After a full day of bonding with these dogs it was close to torture to have to load them onto the bus knowing that they may be put to sleep because they weren't adopted.

One medium to small sized dog that we had was named Midge. She looked to be a mix of maybe a miniature pincher (mini-pin) and something else. She was bigger than a mini-pin but smaller than a beagle. Midge was one of our sad dogs of the day. The reason she was in the shelter was that her owners could not afford to feed her. That was the God's honest truth. Midge was all bones. She had a severe indentation where her hips were, and we could see her bones in her back and her ribs were really obvious. She had the sweetest face and was the most docile little dog you could ever want to meet. The volunteer who was holding Midge all day was a nurse named Mary. Mary was a super kind, super soft spoken, super gentle person. She worked in a hospital with sick children, and it was just her nature to be kind and helpful to the underdog.

When a volunteer holds onto a dog all day, that volunteer develops a bond with that dog. It becomes personal. When people make remarks about the dog, that too becomes personal. Sometimes it makes us happy but sometimes it can really upset us, as was the case with Midge and Mary. Everyone who looked at Midge said things that weren't kind. Over and over Mary would approach prospective adopters and try to get them to see beyond Midge's scrawny appearance and to look deep into her sad eyes and give her a home. Each time they were met with rejection. Towards the end of the day Mary was really beginning to feel defeated, when along came these prospective adopters checking out Midge. For a moment, Mary's hopes were up. She felt that there might be a possibility of them taking Midge home. Much to her disappointment the people said that they thought Midge was "ugly." This exchange took place by the raffle table which was being manned by another wonderful volunteer named Margie. When Margie and Mary heard the "ugly" remark, they both began to cry. Neither one of them saw Midge as ugly. It baffled them that anyone could say such a thing about this poor, sad, neglected pooch.

When I say that these events are emotional for my volunteers I don't lie. Midge did not get a home that day and was put back on the bus. Mary, Margie and I all cried. Midge was a really gentle soul who was so deserving of a good home, not being put back into the cold uncomfortable cage. We couldn't get Midge out of our minds for quite some time after the event and that is one of the prices we pay when we get involved in this type of work.

So many people come up to me and say that they would like to be involved but that they can't "do" what I "do" for that very reason. They can't handle the end of the day when it's time to say goodbye; time to load those disappointed animals back onto a bus that is headed, in many cases, to their deaths. I do understand because I find it to be emotionally exhausting. But when it comes right down to it, I just really want to say, "Suck it up, Nancy," as the father on *Everybody Loves Raymond* says. We can choose to do something or to do nothing. The choice is ours. But isn't it better to choose to save at least some lives as opposed to no lives? If we think of it in those terms, maybe it makes the distastefulness of it a little more bearable.

Midge's story did not have a happy ending. At the next event I asked one of the ladies from the ACC what happened to Midge. She just put her head down, hesitated for a minute and then gave me the sad cold fact. Midge was put to sleep. What a really big injustice this was. That dog, fattened up a little, would have been a perfect dog to be adopted out, but sadly so many people were so shallow and were so into good looks that not one person attending our event could see the beauty that was right before them!

We also had a Lhasa named Herbie at that event. Herbie was a blonde color and needed a good haircut and bath. He was a very cute fellow and at seven years old was not happy to be in a shelter. My friend Carrie and her husband Al had recently lost their wonderful Cocker Spaniel and were hoping to find something to help them not feel so sad. When they saw Herbie they thought he was adorable. Thankfully they could see beyond his knots and sloppy fur. They saw what an adorable little man he truly was. After spending some time with Herbie they decided that he was the boy for them. They filled out the paperwork and loaded Herbie into their expensive car. Herbie was a lucky fellow. Carrie and Al were well-to-do, lived in a very nice home, loved animals and were so kind. Herbie's days of sadness and crappy shelter conditions were behind him!

The next morning I got a call from Carrie. She was a little concerned. They had taken Herbie to be groomed, and he came out adorable. Then they brought him to the vet. It turned out that Herbie was not a healthy pooch. He had a urinary tract infection, an ear infection and a real attitude problem. It cost them $700 at the vet. But she was not complaining about they money, she wasn't complaining that he was *not* at all housebroken and was peeing all over the place, but she *was* complaining about him snarling and biting them! This adorable little fellow with a beautiful hairdo had turned into a terrorist! Herbie would hide under the bed and when they would walk by or try to get him out he would bite them. If they tried to put his leash on he'd allow that, but when it came time to take it off, he'd bite them. When Herbie bit, he broke the skin. Carrie was beside herself. She had never had a dog behave like that before. What was wrong with him? I had no answer for her. I said that perhaps he needed time to learn to trust her. Maybe he was abused, and he is afraid you guys are going to hit him or treat him badly. Give it time. That was all I could offer. A week passed and I got another call with Carrie crying on the other end. Herbie was too vicious, and they had decided that they couldn't work with him. They were actually afraid of him because when he growled and lunged at them to bite, he meant business. Herbie had to be returned to the shelter.

Carrie cried like a baby. I spent some time on the phone with her reassuring her that she had done all she could have done and that if he couldn't be trusted not to bite, then it was going to be impossible to keep him. She was afraid to tell the shelter staff why she was returning him because she didn't want to see him euthanized. I told her that she had to be honest with them and that possibly they would have some way of dealing with a dog like Herbie. I honestly didn't think that they would, but I was grasping at straws trying to ease some guilt from Carrie's mind. I also felt bad that this hellish dog cost her $700 for the vet, $95 for the adoption and $50 for the grooming. Herbie was an expensive disappointment.

After she returned Herbie to the shelter, I called the shelter to plead Herbie's case. I asked them to try to give him another chance. Much to my shock, they had a group that was called New Hope that worked with dogs with issues. So the good folks from New Hope found another group to work with Herbie at their facility. I never followed up on Herbie but hoped that the poor little dude was able to work out his demons and become a good boy.

When we have a case like Herbie, it also is very stressful. I like to be supportive to my adopters as much as I can. If I could work miracles for them in order for their adoptions to be a perfect match, I would. It means the world to me when I hear that an adoption went flawlessly! But every once in a while we end up with a Herbie story, and it is not fun to hear about or to address. Thankfully the Herbie stories are few and far between!

Many other adoptions went smoothly that day, but it was the ones that went bad or didn't happen at all that for some reason seemed to stick out the most in my mind. I guess I was fairly spoiled with the previous three events and all of those adoptions working out so well, that when we hit a big bump in the road it was more than a little upsetting.

When I talk about these events I don't really mention much about the great cats that we successfully adopt out. There is a good reason for that. At these events, I don't get to spend much time with the cats because I am too busy running the show outside of the bus. The cats never get unloaded because it would be too traumatic, so they stay on the bus in their cages and the volunteers take them out when asked. Pat is more the cat person than me, so she runs the show on the bus, making sure that we have enough volunteers helping out with the cats and trying to make sure that the right cat goes to the right home. Pat is wonderful with cats and goes above and beyond to make certain that the fit is right. She has a real knack for judging the feline personality very quickly and can tell almost immediately if the person looking at the cat will be the right match. I admire this skill. I like cats and have four of my own that I love, but I am more the dog *expert.*

SPRING 2005

Boo Boo

THERE IS AN area of Brooklyn called Sunset Park. It is the next town over from Bay Ridge, so to speak. Sunset Park is an area with gorgeous brownstones and big old trees lining many of the streets. While the homes in this area have gotten super expensive and the flavor of the area has started to change, there are still some seedy pockets in the neighborhood. This is the story of BooBoo, a truly loveable Rottweiler-mix pup who really needed to be saved from his grossly abusive, drunk owner.

A woman named Cynthia called me crying one day. She had gotten my name from a co-worker and felt confident that I could help her with BooBoo. Her neighbor, also a Spanish woman, owned this pup. The problem was, she was a raging, violent drunk and beat the poor dog senseless when she was drinking. Cynthia couldn't bear to witness the beatings any more. This woman had a pup earlier in the year that she threw out after it "wasn't cute anymore." The dog was killed by a car. BooBoo was at that "no longer cute" stage and it was his turn to be tossed out like trash. But he didn't want to leave. Even the awful home life he had was more appealing to him than being outside on the street alone; so he just sat there, in front of this tenement like building, waiting to be let back inside. Cynthia couldn't stop crying. She was distraught about what this dog had endured and how this woman was tossing him out into the world to have God knows what happen to him.

Cynthia spoke with BooBoo's owner and begged her to hold onto the dog until she could find him a home. The woman agreed, but all while hung her grossly overweight body out the front window of this slummy building and asked everyone who passed if they wanted a dog. She didn't care who took the dog, she just didn't want him. When I got the call from Cynthia I could hear in her voice how frantic she was. I wasn't sure what I could do for her and told her I would call her back. Hmmm . . . re-homing a seven month old Rotti-mix that is not housebroken and has no manners is not as easy as it sounds. I began to call around and was not having any luck. It was about 6:00 p.m. on a May evening, and everyone I called was either gone for the day, not picking up their phone or just not interested. Within a half hour I got another call from Cynthia. BooBoo's owner was beating him and had thrown him out again. The situation was really bad. So I promised her I would continue to make some calls and that I would be in touch as soon as possible. Finally, I was able to get a pet-sitter to agree to hold onto him for me until I was able to find him a home or bring him to the next adoption event, whichever came first. It would cost me a small fortune, but what could I do? The alternative was to spend a few weeks trying to find him a home and in the meantime run the risk of him being brutalized or given to the wrong people or hit by a car—none of which was an option.

I called Cynthia back and told her I would see her at 7:30 p.m. She gave me the address. She lived next door and would get the dog for us when we got there. I was to call her when I was outside. I couldn't get myself to go by myself for many reasons, but mainly because I was afraid I might assault the owner of the dog! I needed someone rational to go with me and keep me focused on our mission: rescue the dog and good riddance to the owner. I called my buddy Kiki, and she agreed to join me. When we pulled up to the disgusting, neglected old building, I called Cynthia. She instantly appeared in the doorway of the house next door. She gave me a quick, nervous smile and signaled for me to wait a minute while she went into the building next door to get BooBoo. Unbeknownst to me and Kiki, the fat slob that was hanging out the window was the beast that had been abusing BooBoo. As we stood there waiting, we saw Cynthia walk into the apartment and begin speaking Spanish to that imposing figure in the window. Within a minute, out came Cynthia with a terrified BooBoo on a crummy red leash. He was so terrified that she couldn't get him down the steps to come into my car. He was a big pup, about sixty pounds and had a big scar running across the snout. My heart broke as I read the fear in this dog's eyes. I told Cynthia to stop pulling him and to let me come over and talk to him. I slowly approached him and began to talk to him in my high-pitched, "Do you need a mommy, little boy?" voice. I told him that he was a good boy and how handsome I thought he was. I seemed to be able to put him a little at ease. Cautiously, he got into my car. The slob that owned him didn't even say goodbye to him or wish him well. She cracked a toothless smile to us as we put him into the car and that was all the interaction we had with her.

Kiki, who is a petite person, was not comfortable sitting in the back seat of the car with him, so she drove and I comforted him. Once we got to the corner and made a turn, he began to lick my face and his whole body seemed to relax. He knew. He understood that we were friends and that we were going to make sure that nothing bad ever happened to him again. As we drove along, we had to stop at my house to pick up a crate to bring to the dog-sitter. She wasn't willing to take the chance of him doing his business all over her apartment while she was out, so this was part of our agreement. As we continued on our journey, he gradually became a different dog. By the time we got to the dog-sitter's apartment building, rang the bell and brought him up the two flights to her apartment, he wasn't nervous or anxious at all. Instead, he became a happy, strong-willed pup that wanted to have fun. He immediately ran into the bedroom, grabbed a small stuffed animal from the bed and came out with it happily hanging from his mouth. I thought it was so funny; the dog-sitter didn't share my feelings. Unlike me, she was stern and believed in teaching dogs manners.

I called the next day only to find out that BooBoo was not house-broken at all, and understood no commands. She could say sit till she was blue in the face. He didn't know to give the paw, and it looked as though it was going to be a long couple of days for her. From the way

Patricia was talking, I felt like I should give her combat pay for taking in such an unruly dude. I was worried and tried desperately to find him a home. No takers. I held my breath each day hoping that Patricia wouldn't call and ask me to take him because he was so impossible. It wasn't until days later that we realized that poor BooBoo only "hable Espanol." He had no idea what we were saying to him because his owner spoke to him in only Spanish!

As the days passed, the reports got better instead of worse. I was really happy about that. Patricia was taking him to the park to run off some of his energy, and she had gotten him almost completely housebroken in about a week, and she was teaching him English. We agreed that Patricia would bring him to the adoption event and would screen any potential adopters. The day came and Patricia and BooBoo showed up. Patricia immediately began to cry. She had gotten so attached to this handsome guy that the thought of giving him away was killing her. BooBoo was really attached to her as well. I could see by the way he looked at her that he appreciated all that she had done for him and that he enjoyed that new feeling of being loved. He was thriving because of the effort and patience that Patricia had given him.

Finally someone was interested in BooBoo. They seemed like an ideal fit. They had a home with a backyard and had had dogs in the past. Sadly, Patricia agreed to allow them to adopt him. She cried hysterically as she exchanged phone numbers with them and handed them his favorite toy. It was really emotional for all of us to watch, and the poor dog stood there so confused. What was all the crying about? When it was time for him to leave with his new mommy, the look of fear in his face made me cry too. He had no idea why he was being taken away by someone else, but made it very clear that he didn't want to go. He became very stubborn and didn't want to walk with them. Patricia's heart was being ripped apart. She felt like the biggest schmuck on earth. Finally, she agreed to walk to their house with BooBoo so it wouldn't be a traumatic walk for him. She went, said her goodbyes and cried the whole way back to her apartment. She called everyday to make sure that all was well, secretly holding out hope that they wouldn't want to keep him for some reason. She wanted him back in the worst way. As the week came to an end, she began to give up hope. All seemed to be going fine, and it looked as though BooBoo had a new forever home. But then, the call came. They decided that he was too rough for their autistic brother and too much work, so they didn't want him after all. Patricia couldn't get there quick enough to reclaim her little man. She was so happy when she got to take his leash and walk him back to his real home. A home that he would have forever with her!

I didn't know any of this until about a month later when I met her on the avenue and asked if she knew how he was doing. She then explained to me all that had transpired and was glowing as she told me how smart he was and how much work she was putting into teaching him things. They were both having a great time at the park every single day and going for rides in the car with her friend. BooBoo ended up being doted on and treated like a king. About four months later, at another adoption event, Patricia came by with BooBoo to say hello. At first I just looked at him, not realizing who he was, and thought, *what a gorgeous dog*. He had the shiniest coat, the happiest face and the most well behaved demeanor. It was only when I looked at who was holding the leash that I realized that that handsome fellow was my boy, Boo-Boo. Goosebumps covered my body when I thought about how far my little friend had come and how lucky he was that Cynthia made that call on his behalf.

SUMMER 2005

The Dog Days of Summer Adoption Event

BY THE TIME we were hosting the "Dog Days of Summer" event, we felt like we could write a how-to manual for these things! We were good and getting better and better. The effort involved in successfully expediting one of these events was huge. We always seemed to have to work until 10:00 or 11:00 p.m. the night before doing things like making posters, loading the car with all the equipment—the water, dog biscuits, bringing crates with us to show un-wanted or stray neighborhood kittens in, litter-boxes, litter, etc. No one had any idea what went on behind the scenes before these events. There was so much thought involved. This particular month we were on cloud nine because the local paper had done a front page story promoting our upcoming event. The circulation of the paper was 20,000, so we were pretty confident that this would really help boost our results. Not to mention that so many more people would be calling us to leave their names and numbers if they couldn't attend but wanted a pet anyway; that meant more love connections.

Because this event had a summer theme we had a great time shopping for decorations and items to play up the theme. We bought the prettiest, most colorful tablecloths we could find. Then we bought colorful children's sand buckets with little shovels and filled them with candy and placed them on each table. Since we had such beautiful grounds to work with at the church, we bought twenty-five colorful and pretty pinwheels to play up the space. Twenty-five of them allowed us a great spread across the lawn. God blessed us with a soft breeze, making the pinwheels a huge attraction! Add balloons to the pinwheels and we had a carnival like environment. To add a splash more color to the event, I had my volunteers dressed in lime green "Adopt a Shelter Pet" t-shirts and the dogs were all outfitted in matching bandanas as they got off the bus! We were a well- oiled machine!

At each event we have some "visitors." These same "visitors" come religiously to every event. At the church, one of the very first "visitors" is always a man in his 50s with his beautiful Maltese, Benny. Benny is the cutest, whitest, softest Maltese I have ever seen. He has a wonderful disposition and seems to enjoy seeing all the other dogs. When Benny arrived this particular morning, he did his usual stroll across the lawn. We had just inserted the pinwheels into the ground. Much to Benny's dismay, he was smaller in height than our pinwheels. At first he didn't know what to make of them and was a little cautious. After a little investigating he soon realized that they were harmless and that they served a purpose. He walked up to each one and raised his leg. Who needed a fire hydrant when there were pinwheels! The little booger didn't miss one! Benny was on a long, retractable leash and his owner was busy chatting, so he had no idea what Benny was up to—making it even more comical. That day Benny got a nickname—Benny the Urinator—never met a pinwheel he didn't like.

The weather was perfect. We had purchased water bowls for the dogs and had placed them all around the perimeter of the lawn. The dogs drank only Poland Spring at our events and good for them. We also made a point of having plenty of treats on hand for the dogs. They deserved treats. Who knew the next time they would have a treat if they were sent back to the shelter. For all we knew we could be giving them their last treat. I hated to think about it that way but, unfortunately, that was the reality of it. So treat, treat, treat away!

Inside the parish house once again we were serving Brooklyn bagels with the works, coffee, tea, water and plenty of sweet pastry. While making my rounds around the grounds to ensure that things were going smoothly and that all the dogs had bandanas on, I came across a very familiar face. The man stopped me and asked me specifically for a large dog. The breed didn't matter, but it had to be large. I knew it was a face that I had had a previous encounter with, but for whatever reason I couldn't quite figure out when and where. It irked me something awful. I usually can remember that kind of stuff with no problem. As I continued on my way, I replayed in my head what he had said to me. That voice! I knew I had heard it before, and it wasn't a good exchange, but what was it? That's when it hit me like a ton of bricks. The face belonged to a shoemaker that I had given a dog to ten years before. I despised this man. I had found a Shepherd pup, around ten months old, and I had kept him for about a month before deciding that three dogs over seventy pounds was too much to keep in a five room apartment. I named the pup Max and became very attached to him. Ten years ago I wasn't nearly as involved with placing animals as I am now. Back then if I found two or three strays a year that was a lot.

When I decided to put Max up for adoption I posted signs. The shoemaker responded. I met with him, and he assured me that he had had Shepherds in the past and that he loved dogs. I made him promise that if for any reason the dog didn't work out that he would call me—I didn't care if it was one hour from then or ten years, but that he would keep my name and number and let me know if he ever had any problems. He said yes to everything I said to him. So when I left Max with him I didn't feel like I had anything to worry about. I called him the next day and was assured all was well. I let a week go by and I called again. He said that the dog barked too much. Barked too much? I couldn't understand that at all. Max never barked when he was with me.

I called the following week and was told that he had given Max away. I was crushed. To whom and why? I was furious. It turned out that he gave Max to a friend that owned a used car lot, and Max was now living the life of an outdoor dog watching over a bunch of cars! I demanded that he get the dog back from his friend and return him to me immediately. I reminded him of our agreement and of the promises he made to me. He flat out refused. To add insult to injury, he wouldn't tell me where the dog was! Unfortunately, there was absolutely nothing

I could do about this so I had to let it go, but I never forgot what he did to my boy Max!

When I realized who he was I felt like I had been kicked in the gut! I blurted out at the top of my lungs, "Hey you! Aren't you the shoemaker?" To which he nodded his head yes. He didn't remember me or at least he pretended not to. I then took the opportunity to refresh his memory, in a firm voice. I told him that he would *never, ever* get another dog from me and that he should leave my event immediately! I then walked around and made a point of pointing him out to all of my volunteers, making sure that they knew he was *not* to get a dog, today or ever!

The shoemaker disappeared for a short time but then came back, this time with his punk teenage son. Again I made a point of telling him that there was *not* a way in the world that he was getting a dog and that he and his son were wasting their time.

As is the case with most events we always get those one or two dogs that we are certain will be adopted out immediately, and then, much to our surprise, they don't get adopted or get adopted out at the last minute. At this event we had a beautiful white cocker spaniel with little beige freckles on his nose. His name was Smokey, and he was the cutest thing I had seen that day! Smokey's paperwork said he was two years old and owner surrendered because they were moving. We could see that Smokey was not happy about the bus ride he had just had and even less happy to be around so many new people and other dogs. He was *just there,* just his body. His heart and happiness was someplace else. His eyes lacked any spark or excitement and his body language said he was depressed. He didn't wag his tail for anyone and was just moping around all day. Smokey did absolutely nothing to help sell himself.

As the day wore on, each time I'd pass by Smokey I'd lean over and softly chat with him. I'd say things like, "Smile handsome fellow, please! Just give a little wag of the tail! Come on buddy, we're on your side. We want you to have a new mommy just as badly as you want to have a new mommy. Please little man, work with me." I'd then pet his soft little head, touch his long, velvety ears and offer him a biscuit which he would never take. The day passed, and no one took him. The volunteer holding him was so sad. It was her first event, and she had such high hopes of Smokey going home, so needless to say there were tears shed. As I tell anyone who volunteered and had a day end that way, "We tried! What more can we do?" I only wish that Smokey's previous owners could have been made to sit through this painful day, that they could have felt the sadness that their dog emanated all day.

People who just surrender their dogs to the shelter without any thought of what the dog will be feeling or thinking should have their conscience rattled with a reality check! Smokey didn't deserve to be put in a shelter. He should have been re-homed by his owners, but I guess accepting that responsibility was too much for them. They should be made to stand in the driveway of the church and forced to listen to the desperate sounds that come from the dogs when the doors on the bus close, and it begins to make that sad, painful journey back to the shelter. Perhaps that would help make them think about something other than the quick, easy fix of doing the good old "owner surrender."

SUMMER AND FALL 2005

Homeless in Brooklyn

THERE'S AN EXPRESSION that goes like this: "Brooklyn, only the strong survive." I have to admit that Brooklyn is a place like no other, filled with a big cast of characters. Lately we are seeing many homeless on the streets of Bay Ridge. I guess if I were to become a homeless person in Brooklyn, the streets of Bay Ridge would be my choice. Bay Ridge boasts a very eclectic mix of people. We go from middle class to super rich within a matter of blocks. We have a very safe community and a beautiful, small town type of environment. I believe that the small town feel is one of the reasons our neighborhood is so safe. Everyone knows everyone else, kind of like the TV show *Cheers*.

One of our "usuals" is an older fellow named Mike. He has been on the streets for about three years now. In the summer he has the most wonderful tan from being outdoors. Whenever we see this poor soul, he is sitting uncomfortably in the side doorway of a Rite Aid drug store. He walks with a cane and has pain etched in his face. Mike never asks for money and always has a quick smile and hello if someone makes eye contact with him, which most people don't. For some reason, our youngest dog, Nuggie, loves Mike. She insists on going over to him each time she sees him and rolling over on her back so he can pet her belly. Nuggie doesn't care that his hands are filthy and smelly and that he reeks to high heaven. All Nuggie sees is that this is someone who smiles at her and that, to her, is an invitation to come over and be his buddy for a few moments. The way Mike smiles when he sees her and how happy he appears to be when he pets her makes me get all choked up. If Mike were a stray dog, more people would look kindly upon him and want to help him. But, as a "stray" human, the opposite holds true.

Some people have said to me that it's gross that we allow Nuggie to say hello to Mike. Gross!? I think it is wonderful for both Mike and Nuggie that they have the chance to appreciate each other. Mike probably doesn't get to express affection to anyone these days and doesn't seem to have anyone expressing affection towards him, but Nuggie does. She doesn't see anything wrong with Mike and looks forward to their meetings. Now, Sal and I frequently make a point of getting him a bagel and coffee when we see Mike in the mornings. I don't know what brought Mike to this point, but I do know that he is a kind-faced man who is down on his luck, and it takes nothing for me and my husband to allow our dog to give him some love while we are out on our walks. So in my mind, my "Baby Nuggie" gets two thumbs up for being unconditionally accepting!

Spare a Quarter? Nice Dog

One of the newest additions to our homeless ranks is a very heavyset, forty-ish fellow with curly hair. I began to see him over the summer, and he would wear these huge wide-legged blue shorts and Hawaiian shirts and sandals. When he first started to hang around the neighborhood he was bag-less and just had what he was wearing—no belongings. Each time I would meet him, he'd say, with a bit of a Southern twang, "Spare a quarter?" Of course the first few times I did, but then I began to see him rolling joints and saying, as he rolled, "Spare a quarter?" As the months passed, he began to acquire comforters and bags that he carried around with him. He picked up a red wagon from the garbage and that helped him carry all his stuff.

The interesting thing about this guy was that he was always drinking a grande Starbucks coffee and rolling a joint. If I was doing the math correctly, it took an awful lot of quarters to get a grande Starbucks coffee and a joint. I mentioned to Sal one day that this guy was never without a joint. He said he hadn't noticed. I told him to pay attention next time he saw him. Sure enough, the next day Sal came into the office chuckling. He had just bumped into "Spare a quarter?" and sure enough he was rolling a joint.

As the summer changed to fall, "Spare a quarter?" was still calling the benches on Third Avenue home, and he was really annoying the neighbors. He would just stop mid-stride, turn toward the curb and pee into the street or tree-well. He didn't care who was around or even if he splashed anyone. One of my neighbors was so disgusted watching him do this repeatedly right across from her living room window that she called the police on him. When she told me the story, I said that I hadn't seen him do that yet, but I knew it was just a matter of time. Sure enough, one freezing cold evening in early December, I was waiting for someone to pick me up so we could help decorate the local park for a holiday party. I was standing outside my office on busy Third Avenue when out of the corner of my eye I caught a glimpse of his massive body. Sure enough, just as my neighbor had described, he stopped mid-stride, turned slightly toward the street and began to pee. There was a woman sitting in a car double-parked just a few feet from his stream. She had a bird's eye view. I, on the other hand, was standing across the street just chuckling to myself.

"Spare a quarter?" was an incredibly sloppy homeless guy and so grossly overweight he looked to have never missed a meal or a snack. He started to camp out on the benches, and each time I saw him he was surrounded by all sorts of sandwich wrappings, empty chip bags, soda bottles and of course his trademark Starbucks coffee and joint. One morning as I was walking to the office I passed him by. As he sat rolling a joint at 10:00 a.m., he spewed his usual "Spare a quarter?" phrase at me. This time, for whatever reason, I just had to respond. I looked at him and said, "You know, if you stopped smoking so much pot, you'd have a whole lot of quarters" and then kept going. As I continued on my way, he yelled to my back, with his Southern drawl, "Ya know, I gotta drinking problem too." It's amazing all the habits he could support with quarters.

When we met him with the dogs, his rap was a little different. It went more like, "Spare a quarter? Nice Dogs"—all in one breath. For some reason Nuggie senses that there is something different about him, perhaps it's the pot smell, but luckily she doesn't have any inclination to visit with him.

MONSTER'S STORY

MONSTER IS OUR six year old Lhasa. He came named and, since he responded to it, we decided to keep it. He is an adorable furry-faced pooch but, like my husband says, he has issues, big ones. I saved Monster from a hell-hole shelter four years ago. Poor little fellow had been held hostage there for fourteen months and, because of that, he is extremely damaged in many ways.

He has a very bad anxiety based barking condition. Once he starts, he doesn't stop. I keep telling him he's lucky that I'm the landlord because no one would rent to us! In addition to this wacky barking stuff, he has food issues. Now, who among us doesn't, but his food issues make me sad when I think of why they exist. During those fourteen long months that Monster was in the shelter, he was kept in a small cage. The cage had about two inches of space between the floor, where his feet actually touched, and the poop pan that was in place under it. Because Monster would get so excited about getting fed, he would knock over his food bowl, and all of the dry food would fall into the poop tray below! As a result, my little man went without food many times, as did his shelter mates. As a result of this kind of treatment, this troubled little fellow is a stealth thief. He steals cat food at every opportunity and has been stealing Nuggie's food since she joined us. He is so fast that his little furry face almost makes a suction cup effect with the food dish, and he is able to somehow inhale all the contents in a matter of seconds. It is like nothing I have ever seen before and, while sometimes it is funny, the reality of it is sad. After four years with us, my little pea-brain dude still thinks he may be starved to death, so he has to grab whatever he can!

Monster also has an obsession with eating clothing. He loves to steal clothing and to eat large pieces out of it. He has stolen multiple pajama tops belonging to me and has eaten eight inch circles out of them, all in one piece. It is the most incredible thing. Somehow he manages to chew a perfectly round hole into an article of clothing and swallows it in one piece. We have been very lucky so far, because usually after two or three days he will either throw up the entire thing in one piece or he will poop it out. But while waiting for these "results" we are nervous wrecks for fear that his intestines are going to get strangled or that the intestines will get infected.

We try to be diligent about keeping any pieces of clothing out of his reach but every once in a while we will forget or we will catch the little wise guy standing up on his back legs trying to grab hold of something with his teeth, ever so slowly pulling it down to the ground. Because he is so adorable, we can't get mad at him, not that it would do any good anyway.

Monster loves to dig, so we have to keep sheets on all of our living room furniture. If we didn't, our couch and chair would be threadbare. Over the past few months, he has decided to try to eat the sheets. We don't own one sheet that doesn't have a hole in it. At this point, we have realized that the person who named Monster was right on the money and that they must have spent some time with him before naming him because he truly is a little Monster.

Monster loves to cuddle and is desperate for attention. He requires constant petting at night when we sit down to watch TV. He always wants to be sitting with us and will roll all around on his back trying to make sure that his belly is getting rubbed. I think that he is trying to compensate for all the time that he spent confined to that terrible wire cage. My husband is truly wild about "his little dude" and is more than happy to indulge him each evening. When the two of them sit on the couch together they have such a great time; all the while both of them make the silliest noises.

The arm of my couch has become Monster's "post." He thinks he's a security guard, and I am tempted to get a little blue uniform shirt made for him, but he'd probably eat it. Every chance he gets, he positions himself there. As long as he sits there he can see anyone coming or going from our home and the neighbor's house. He lets out these deep growling sounds and barks insanely if someone so much as hesitates in front of our house. He thinks he is a tough guy, and I do believe that is because he knows that Gallagher has his back. When we walk Monster solo, he is friendly, outgoing and a nice little fellow. Pair him up with Gallagher and Nuggie, he becomes "The Arnold" of dogs!

Unfortunately, Monster also had a terrible medical condition. Calcium oxylate crystals built up in his bladder. This required an expensive, gruesome surgery to fix. The recuperation period was horrible. He was in agony. He had been on a special diet to try to ensure he didn't have this problem again—and there we were, three years later and he was urinating blood again! I was sick over it. Sal brought him to the vet, and they gave us a specimen cup to get a urine sample from him. Sounded easy enough, right . . .

On the way home from the vet Sal tried to get a sample. He managed to get about four droplets of bloody urine. That's it. He came into the house and showed me the cup with the droplets. Then he asked if I thought that it was enough. Of course it wasn't enough—we needed at least an inch in the bottom of the cup—in my *expert opinion*. So, after having Monster home for about a half hour, we took him in the yard to see if we could get some more. No luck, the little wise-guy picked up his leg at lightening speed, so by the time we bent over and positioned the cup, the pee was already running down the bark of the tree. Okay, we'd have to try again later . . .

Saturdays were hectic for us. I had to go to work, and Sal had to give guitar lessons. So I decided that it would be "take your bad boy to work day"—which meant bringing Monster to work with me and periodically walking him with hopes of getting some more urine for our sample. Sal came to the office during a break he had. Together we set out on bustling Third Avenue armed with our specimen cup—we were on a mission. No luck. Okay, we'd try on the next break.

The next time, we set out with a disposable cup figuring it was a little bigger, and we might be able to catch more urine with the opening being wider than the specimen cup. Still no luck. The little booger doesn't pee much during each squirt. It turned out that was why he lifted his leg on everything as we walked—because each squirt was really just a few drops or sometimes, as we soon found out, just essence—nothing comes out—just his good wishes! So there we were again—chasing after him with this bright red cup coaxing him to do pee-pee on the objects we thought would be most conducive to us making a successful collection: hydrants, poles, trees and the delivery boy's bike next door.

This had become a real production! There we were, on this busy avenue, not even thinking about how silly we must have looked, and better yet, sounded! Still, we had no luck. We agreed that we would try again on Sal's next break . . .

Sal came over again and this time we decided to bring with us a small bowl. The mouth of the bowl was so large that we figured there was no way we could fail. Never say never. Once again we set out on the bustling avenue. Here it was. A picture perfect Saturday afternoon, everyone running their errands; after all, we have the bank, dry cleaner, supermarket, pharmacy and hardware store all right here. So there we were again, like two morons, saying in our cutesy voices, "Come on Monster, pee-pee . . . Come on little dude . . . Gooood Boyyyy!" Sure the mouth of the bowl was big, but when Monster finished peeing, he put his leg down so quickly that his paw landed right into our bowl. In addition to spilling the very little urine we were able to collect all over my fingers, we now had all the dirt from his paw mixed in. How good of a sample could we possibly have gotten? After all of this hoopla, we still were only successful in gathering about one teaspoon of pee, which we brought to the vet with hopes that it was good enough—otherwise, we would have to find more creative ways of getting this sample. It turned out that we had enough, mission accomplished, finally!

Monster and YiaYia

My in-laws live next door to us; our homes are attached. For six months out of the year they live in Greece. In the winter of 2004, while I was doing some extensive renovations on my house, Monster would continually bark at the contractors. He was making everyone nuts! One day my mother-in-law, Vicky, suggested that she take him next door with her for the day. I reluctantly agreed because she was not a dog lover and had never been around dogs. But I was so fed up with the little freak barking, and making the other two bark, that I agreed. Throughout the day, she would drop by to tell me how cute my boy was and how much fun she was having with him. I found this to be very amusing, coming from a non-dog-liking person. The next day the work was continuing on the house, and Vicky again offered to take my bad boy for the day. I was only too happy to have him out of my way. He was a real trouble maker, always making everyone else bark.

This quickly became her routine. Each morning she would take her "Agoraki," which means little boy in Greek. She was quickly falling for him! Vicky thought that everything he did was adorable, even the way he pooped! Through her broken English, she would explain to me what good "care" she was taking of him. When he'd come in from the yard after peeing or pooping, she'd clean his paws with a warm, damp cloth. She had gotten him so conditioned to this that he would now stand still at the door waiting for her to come with the towel and then would give her each paw to clean! This was remarkable because ordinarily he was the most un-cooperative little fellow around. He was a pampered Prince with YiaYia—Greek for Grandma! He was "company" for her as she liked to tell me.

He certainly had been successful at lifting her spirits. Vicky was only in her late fifties and suffered from the empty nest syndrome. She was the ultimate Mom/Caretaker. That was what she did, care for people—her husband and her children. But now, with her two children married and out of the house, her caretaking abilities were much less in demand and she hated that. Having never worked outside the home and not able to speak much English, she needed to be needed. Monster was needy, and she enjoyed being needed by him! Prior to Monster becoming her "Agoraki," she cried easily and was always complaining about some ache or pain. Now, with Monster in her world, she was pain free and so happy—all the time!

From January through May of 2004, Monster spent from 8 a.m. to 10 p.m. with YiaYia. He loved the attention. Every morning she'd call and ask me to "send me my boy." He soon began to understand that when the phone rang in the morning, it was *YiaYia time.* So, without me saying a word, he'd run to the back door and do his little rat-tat-tat dance until he heard her lock click open. Then he would take off like a speed demon down the steps. My father-in-law had opened the fence between the two yards so he had easy access, spoiled boy that he had become.

Monster was happy with this new arrangement because from early morning till late at night, he got 100% attention. He never got tired of being petted or picked up. Because Vicky liked to knit, Monster had the most gorgeous wardrobe. The handmade sweaters this little dude sported on our walks were quite the conversation piece. She even made little girly sweaters for Nuggie with matching bonnets. We tried to explain to her that dogs don't wear hats, to which she responded with her heavy Greek accent, "It's all right." Each one of Monster's sweaters was monogrammed with a giant M on the back, and he kind of reminded me of Laverne on *Laverne and Shirley.*

As time passed, my father-in-law, Xenophon, who was absolutely *not* a dog person, started to smile at Monster. He saw what an amazing effect Monster was having on his wife. I also don't think he could resist Monster's beautiful little furry face, enormous brown eyes, super long eye lashes and winning disposition! He even began sitting on the floor with Monster and talking Greek baby talk to him. Monster had become the grandchild that they had wanted for years, but easier—no diapers or teething.

Vicky sang Monster Greek nursery rhymes and carried this twenty-five pound little dog around the house. She told me, "Maryzo, he understand me. I think speak Greek." I said, "Yep, that's my boy, bilingual like your son . . ." They'd go on hour long walks together each day. My mother-in-law had never walked around the neighborhood so much in her life. She was so excited to have company to walk with. Each day, as they were headed home from their journey, YiaYia brought Monster to visit me at work. It was so funny and so cute to see that little face at my door, jumping up with his chubby little paws to try to get my attention.

When the time came for them to take their annual trip to Greece, the tears began. For thirty-five years they have taken their extended holidays to Greece. Since Sal was a teenager, he has not been participating in these trips. So when it was time to go, he got a hug and a kiss and was told to behave—and that was it—they were off—gone for months. But now—now there was Monster to say goodbye to. So for two weeks before she left, my mother-in-law cried at the thought of not seeing her "Agoraki." On the day she was scheduled to leave, we could see she had been crying all night. She couldn't bear the thought of not to seeing her boy every day. She came over to say goodbye and sat on the kitchen floor sobbing and holding Monster so tight. She told me to take good care of him, and I told Sal, "I bet you never got that kind of goodbye..." Monster had proven himself to be more powerful than any meds or doctors. I think we should call him Prozac.

For more than a week after YiaYia left, my poor little dude went out in the yard and stood in front of her back door waiting for his favorite sound—the clicking of the lock. He looked so disappointed and so frustrated because despite his adorable rat-tat-tat dance, still there was no YiaYia. He continued to wait patiently and then after a few minutes sadly came back home. Poor little man didn't understand what that whole goodbye ceremony meant . . .

Once in Greece, she called on Saturdays and talked to Monster. His ears perked up and he looked a little confused. It meant the world to her to be able to have her little "chats" with him.

SUMMER 2005

Charlie, Speedy and Mouse

ONE BRUTALLY HOT Tuesday evening in July, I received a call from a woman named Sofie. She was whispering to me on the phone in a voice so low I could hardly hear her. The reason for her call was that she had taken in four four-week old kittens and needed someone to help her with them (i.e. take them off her hands). Even though she was not from the immediate community, she still knew of me and "my works." I got a kick out of these calls. It turned out she was going to keep one of the litter but her screaming husband was in the next room threatening to take the other three to the shelter—at that very moment. In between trying to talk to me, Sofie was begging him not to. I told her to bring them to me at my office, and that I would take care of finding someone to foster them. I had someone in mind and called her. Her name was Stephanie, and she agreed to help. It was all arranged.

About fifteen minutes later, into my office walked a tall, salt and pepper haired man with a box. I asked, "Are you Martin?" His reply was a low grunt. Yep, he was Martin all right. I opened the box and do what every animal loving freak does—I took one of the kittens and nuzzled it right up to my face. As I was doing this, I realized that the kitty had no fur on its tail! I took out the other two and *none* of them had fur on their tails! *Oh no!* I thought. Then I looked at them, and two of the three were missing most of the fur off their little back paws, too. Suddenly, I was itchy. It was all psychological and I knew that, but I still felt itchy! Remember, I was just nuzzling one of these little creatures to my face. Geez! Now what on earth did I do to myself? Think ringworm. I'd never seen it before but had heard horror stories about how "catchy" it was.

I tried to maintain my composure so that I could chat with Martin. He explained to me that his wife was an animal freak like me. I explained to him as quickly as I could what I do. He then told me that he believed his wife would love to get involved with me to help. At this point, I was not going to miss my opportunity—"Well, if helping animals is what your wife really enjoys, then wouldn't it be terrific if she had a husband who was supportive, rather than one who screams threats about shelters in the background while she is on the phone trying to place some little defenseless kitties on a hot summer day?" I continued, "You know, I am only as successful as I am because of my wonderful, supportive husband. He not only encourages me and is proud of me, but he helps out in any way he can." At this point, at least five minutes of chatting had transpired, and I was itching to call the vet, in more ways than one!

The vet's office knew me all too well and immediately gave me an appointment. I flew up there with Pat, who arrived just after Martin left. She never could resist seeing "new arrivals." Upon examining them I was told that they were full of all sorts of "goodies": lice, fleas and ringworm. Now I was really itchy. Not to worry the vet told me—lice were species specific—meaning a cat could only get lice from a cat. Somehow this did not take the itch away. Then came the really good news, it would take five to seven days to get fungus culture results to see if they had ringworm. For me that would be a very long five to seven days. In the meantime, the vet tech agreed to shampoo them for me and keep them overnight while they dried. I was relieved when she offered to hold them overnight because that gave me time to figure out an alternate plan for them.

As I was given the news about the deluxe package of "goodies" that came with these kitties I realized that poor Sofie was keeping one of these fully loaded kitties and that she had a dog and two cats in a one-bedroom apartment. This meant that they were all being exposed. I didn't have her number with me at the vet and had to wait to get back to my office to call her. Needless to say, when I broke the news to her, she flipped out and with a husband like Martin, I'd say with good reason!

I then needed to tell the ready, willing and able foster mommy that I would not be requiring her services—she had cats and two other kittens that she was fostering for me, not to mention three kids, so her fostering was out of the question. All I can say is thank goodness my in-laws went to Greece for six months out of the year and lived next door. Sal and I became the foster mommies for the little "goodie filled" boogers. Sal was such a good mommy and really got into socializing the kitties. Initially we referred to them as the Three Stooges but as we got to know them, we called them Speedy, Mouse and Charlie. We had a ball with them. At some moments, it was like watching an acrobatic show starring wide-eyed, energy filled, silly kitties!

Charlie, Speedy and Mouse were with us for six weeks, and we grew terribly attached to them. Their personalities were so different. Speedy was the biggest of the gang. A gorgeous grey tiger striped fellow with a calendar worthy face. He was so cute he was edible. Speedy was the fastest little fellow I had ever met! When we would open up the door to visit with them, Speedy would *fly* past us and run up the stairs. He was quite the character and too curious for his own good.

Charlie was black and white with a half black moustache, reminding us of Charlie Chaplin. Initially he was the most aloof of the three, but by the end he had become a little lover-boy. Charlie was a bit of a wise guy too and enjoyed playing and getting into trouble, a typical kitty, I suppose. Charlie was the medium sized one of the group and a handsome boy in his own right.

And then there was Mouse. Mouse was everyone's favorite. Anyone who saw the three adored Mouse. There was something really special about his face. He had this really wide-eyed look and terrific patches of bright white whiskers around his eyes and nose. Like his brother Charlie, he was black and white, but more black than white. Mousey was the smallest of the litter and was the Romeo of the group. He loved people. When we would come to feed them the other two would be going crazy for the food. But not Mouse. He'd be trying to climb up my sneaker so that I'd pick him up! If I didn't pay attention to him, he would sit and pat my leg with his paw and meow repeatedly trying to get his message across—"Pick me up!" He loved to be held like a baby and purred super loudly! Both Sal and I had a really hard time parting with him. He was a special boy.

While shacking up in my mother-in-law's house, these wild little fellows got into all sorts of trouble. If my in-laws knew half of what went on with these kittens, they'd want to kill us! So we had to make certain that things looked just as they did when they left or as close as possible, which was more difficult that it sounds. We decided that to keep the kitties in a crate was not fair, so after the first two days of crating, we moved them into the entry hall. This area was about four feet wide and ten feet long and was extremely bright because it faced the front of the house and had an all glass door. It was a terrific space for them because they could see and hear the outside world and what's more, the neighbors could admire them as they walked past.

At the end of this hallway was a door that led into my mother-in-law's dining room/living room area. Because the weather had been extremely humid, the door didn't close completely one day after Sal had done the afternoon feeding. So that evening, when we went over to see the boogers, they were not at the door ready to greet us. That could only mean one thing, and it wasn't good! Sure enough Sal and I were horrified to see the damage these out of control kitties did! It looked like a college kid's hotel room after spring break!

Anyone who knows Greek people know that Greeks love crystal and china pieces. Since my in-laws do not have any pets in the house that climb on furniture, they have lovely crystal pieces on a low coffee table. I should say they had . . . There were pieces of crystal everywhere! The gorgeous, tall crystal vase and five pound crystal ashtray were history! Since the floors are ceramic tile, crystal bouncing on ceramic makes for quite the shatter. The truly remarkable thing was that with all these glass shards on the floor, encompassing a very large area, none of the kitties had gotten even a splinter of glass, Thank God! There was no blood anywhere, and the kitties seemed to be amused with the damage they created.

The destruction did not stop with the broken crystal. On the floor there were two small throw rugs. These beautiful, colorful throw rugs had served as their very first scratching post. Sweet, huh? But wait, it doesn't stop there. The lovely, decorative cushions that adorned my mother-in-law's couch had been knocked down and were now serving as thrones for these three kings! They had also managed to climb up the beautiful *knit* bedspread that was on a guest bed. On their journey up the spread and across it to the other end, they managed to leave pull marks from their nails all over the place. These little freaks made a mess!

The boogers loved to be chased and each day while Sal and I prepared their food we always allowed them into my mother-in-law's apartment to run around for a little while. They loved the freedom of all of the open space! And like clockwork, when it came time for us to leave, we would always have to chase them in order to grab them and put them back in the entry hall. Unfortunately, this time was no different. So, while trying to digest the damage, we were also trying to grab the boogers without them getting cut on the glass! I think I aged ten years in those few moments!

Once the glass was all cleaned up, we then realized that we had to figure out a way to break the news to my mother in-law when she got back. What to do? We decided to do what any two cowards would do. Lie. We told her that her precious Monster came running in to see if YiaYia was home from Greece yet and *he* jumped on the coffee table and knocked everything over and then because he was sad, *he* peed on her throw mats and we threw them away. Since she knows Monster and how spiteful he can be, she could easily swallow this story. And lucky for us, there is nothing in the world she loves more than Monster, so he can do no wrong, ever!

As the boogers began to grow and become more curious, Sal decided to make them a great little kitty condo! He took two boxes and taped them together. He then cut square, rectangular and circular holes in odd places in the boxes. The kitties would spend hours playing in the condo. They had so much fun hiding, sneaking up on each other and boxing with each other through the holes! We enjoyed watching their silly antics from outside. Because they could be seen from the street, some of our animal loving neighbors would stand outside giggling while watching them perform! It soon became part of their routine to stand, laughing outside my mother-in-law's fence, observing the games these kitties played with each other!

We gave the kitties away after six weeks of fostering, and for weeks we found ourselves trying to peek in on them as we passed my mother-in-law's house. Then the reality would hit, the boogers belonged to someone else. Kind of sad for us in one sense, but a job well done in another! Mouse and Charley were taken by the same people and Speedy went to a home with a four month old kitty the same colors as his. The new owners are all friends and promise to allow the kitties to have "play-dates." I guess I can't ask for better than that?

SEPTEMBER 2005

Divorced man finds new love interest

WHEN WE FIRST met Timothy, a thirty-something guy, he was a very depressed fellow who looked so sad. He came into our real estate office as a client. He was unemployed, in the midst of a divorce and heartbroken. He was the one who had to move out of their co-op, and more importantly he was losing custody of their dog and that was killing him. Timothy had a sister who lived far away and both of his parents had passed away; he was feeling really alone.

Sal and I, both having been divorced in the past, gave him a pep talk about life after divorce. That it can be even better than before the divorce, and that I, with two divorces behind me, was living proof that the old adage, "If at first you don't succeed, try, try, try again" works! Within minutes we had him laughing and feeling better about his situation. We were very lucky to find him an apartment that was pet friendly even though he didn't have a pet anymore, and we promised that we would help him out with that too.

Timothy quickly got himself settled into his apartment and was really looking forward to coming to our adoption event the following month. He wanted to adopt a pup that wouldn't get too big, but not a "smalldog." When Timothy arrived at the event, he took one look at this adorable pup and adopted her! Lexington was a delightful little Pit Bull, possibly Collie mix. She was brindle in color and had the softest fur. At four months old, she was full of puppy love, puppy teeth, energy and fun. Timothy was now a very proud daddy to this wonderful little lady. He beamed while he proudly strolled the avenue introducing her to the other four-legged friends in the community. Lexington had gotten Timothy out of the house, talking to people and smiling once again. We could see that he was enjoying her immensely. Being unemployed was actually turning out to be a blessing for Timothy because he had the luxury of time on his hands to bond with his little lady and to housebreak her. Timothy went from a sad Sam to a happy Harry in a few short weeks, and we'd like to think that he owed it all to little Miss Lexington. In the meantime, Lexington was a spoiled beyond belief princess. She was so lucky to have a kind, easy going, good-natured owner like Timothy, and it was my hope that he finds his next wife while walking along the picturesque shore with his new sweetheart, Lexington. After all, she was a chick magnet!

FALL 2005

The I'm Falling For You Adoption Event

THE NIGHT BEFORE this event Pat and I were in my office, deliriously tired, preparing everything for the next morning. As was the case with every event, we always created posters depicting some of the neighborhood pets that needed homes. These pets were either strays that people had rescued or pets that the families could no longer keep. We worked hard to come up with funny, witty stories or sad, sappy stories, depending on each pet's situation. This night we were really feeling punchy. We needed a foster home for a pregnant mother kitty, just until she gave birth and weaned the kitties. Then we'd take her back and place the kitties. We were trying so hard to think of something clever to say, but we were so tired the words just weren't coming. Finally, we came up with, "Knocked up feline seeks place to call home until the buns come out of the oven." We had a picture of the momma-to-be and then a bunch of funny kitty stickers all around the poster. At the bottom it said, "See Pat for tissues . . ." and had a Kleenex affixed to the bottom of the poster. We were roaring with laughter because it came out so well.

Then we had a bunch of cats that needed a foster home because their owner was being evicted. We had the best time coming up with funny ways of telling their story, at the owner's expense of course. We laughed so much that we had tears in our eyes. We just hoped that the owner wouldn't be passing by our event and reading our signs.

We were particularly excited about this day because we had a special treat for everyone, in the form of a "celebrity guest" to help us out. The ASPCA's Assistant Director of Humane Law Enforcement, Joseph Pentangelo, was going to spend the day with us signing autographs and speaking with people about making the right choice when adopting. Joe's wife, Joanne, was also joining us, and she brought along a bunch of handmade bandanas that she had worked with some children on designing for the shelter dogs to wear when we took them off the bus. They were colorful and all had some kind of writings on them, courtesy of these animal loving kids. When Joe and his wife arrived, they brought along one of their own dogs, a Mastiff named Kane that they had rescued. This Mastiff was almost a twin of one of the dogs we ended up having for adoption that day, Muzzie, and much like Muzzie, he was a gentle giant, and everyone was fascinated by his size and striking beauty. My volunteers and the people attending the event were thrilled to meet Joe and Joanne. I was honored and grateful that Joe took time from his busy schedule to spend the day with us.

We were truly blessed with a wonderful, breezy fall day for the adoption event. The prep for this was like the prep for all the others; lots of last minute things to do and a late night of hard work for Pat and me in my office and, as evidenced by our turnout, with literally hundreds of people coming by. Hard work does payoff!

The day started with me bringing Mouse3 with me to the event. Mouse3 was a kitty that was thrown out of her house on the Wednesday night before the event by a miserable man—a whole other story—and my husband and I rescued her and kept her for three days until the event. As we were driving there, Mouse3 was so nervous that she pooped in the carrier. There I was, ready to throw up at any moment, trying to get to the church where the event was being held as fast as I could! As I drove along with all four windows wide open, I was having visions of this kitty sitting and stepping in the poop. It is very hard to adopt out a smelly cat. I was on a mission to get Mouse3 out of that carrier as quickly as I possibly could.

As soon as I arrived at the church, I pulled into the parking lot, jumped from the car and grabbed the dog crate that I had collapsed in my trunk. I tried to open it as quickly as I could but, of course, it gave me a hard time. All the while I am stressing that the kitty is getting agitated and is going to be covered in poop! Finally, I get the darn thing open and transfer Mouse3 into the crate with a litter box. Poor Mouse3 was not happy about that at all. She complained endlessly, which just made me more anxious.

As always, my car was loaded with things for our event. There are so many things necessary to have on hand in order to pull off an event like ours, that my car was filled to capacity. Unfortunately, I was alone so there was no one to help me unload and transport these supplies from the parking lot to the parish house, where we host the crowds. As I unpacked the car and put all the stuff into a neat pile on the side, Mouse3 made her unhappiness even more apparent. She was reaching up to the top of the crate, screaming. I felt like a schmuck. This was a wonderful little five month old black and white kitty who just wanted to roll over and have her belly rubbed. Instead, I had her caged. It made me so sad. I kept telling myself that the kitty was going to get a great home and that I was helping her. I convinced myself that these few moments of discomfort for the kitty were necessary in order to show her off and get her a good home (in the back of my mind I had already decided that if she didn't get taken, that she would end up being kitty number five; like I needed a kitty number five!)

As I was trying to cope with this situation, Frank showed up with Penelope. Penelope was a pup that had been found about a month previously, and Frank and his family had been kind enough to foster her all this time while waiting for the event. Penelope was an adorable pup. At about five months old, her origins were almost impossible to figure out. She was fawn like a Boxer or Rhodesian, but her body was kind of lean and sleek. She had a lovely long, skinny tail, silly ears and a great frown on her forehead. She loved feet. As long as she could curl herself in a ball on someone's feet, she was content. I really thought that this was one terrific little lady, and Frank felt sad saying goodbye to her. He relayed to me what an absolute angel she was and I could see by the way he looked at her that he was feeling bad. I couldn't blame him. Any pet in my possession for more than five minutes owns a special place in my heart, and Frank had this darling little lady for one month. I could see that she owned his!

After Frank and I got acquainted, along came Judy. Judy was a retired school teacher who had called me the night before to ask if she could bring a pup that had been pawned off to a cat rescuer on the street the week prior. The pup was also five months old and a very easy adoption. I had told Judy that she was welcome to bring the pup and that I'd be happy to help place it. So, true to her word, she came bright and early. He was a Poodle mix named Tawney; just a white ball of puff sporting an adorable blue bandana. As we chatted, Penelope and Tawny were getting acquainted with each other. They seemed to understand that they were both sweet, young pups and adjusted to each other immediately. They were very adorable together. Judy and Frank then assisted me in moving all of my stuff inside, including Mouse3 who was had gotten much quieter since the arrival of the dogs.

Judy helped me start to decorate, and we were doing very well. Slowly the other volunteers began to arrive. We were only too happy to have the help. After about a half hour Pat arrived with Mommycat. Mommycat was an adorable kitty herself. At just about nine months old, she had been discarded from a home in beautiful Dyker Heights and put onto the streets to fend for herself. Needless to say, Mommycat ended up pregnant and alone, living off the generosity of some kind neighbors. One neighbor in particular, Virginia, took a special interest in Mommycat and her kitties. She contacted Pat about Mommycat and the babies; slowly but surely, we were able to place all three babies. Sadly, that left Mommycat, still just a baby herself all alone on the street; she seemed so sad, and Virginia felt really awful about her. We tried so hard to get her a home. Virginia even had her fixed and tested to make her an easier placement. After weeks of no success we decided to bring her along to the adoption day too. She was not happy. Having never been in a cage before, this kitty was really acting out. She was hollering for hours. Everyone felt so awful. She was really agitated about what was going on around her, and who could blame her. Everywhere she looked there were dogs and people, and plenty of noise. This poor little lady was overwhelmed and terrified. After many hours at the adoption event, she finally got a home. Everyone who had been trying to comfort her throughout the day was relieved. It was wearing us all down emotionally listening to her shrieks! Being pet lovers, there is nothing more upsetting to us than an unhappy or uncomfortable animal that we can't seem to soothe. We want to make everyone of them happy and as quickly as we possibly can!

Within no time, Tawny was snatched up. One of our volunteers had a friend who had come to the event looking for a small dog, so before the bus even arrived, we had Tawny adopted out. That was the easiest adoption ever.

Then it was time to focus on Penelope. Penelope was so sweet. She had a foot fetish. So whoever was handling her would always have her sitting on their feet because that is where she felt most comfortable. Penelope was dressed in our customary bandana and was being shown on the lawn with all the other pooches. She was an excellent pup and loved everyone. She too was adopted early into the event by a woman name Mirella and the rest is history. She and Penelope hit it off famously. Mirella is a very soft spoken, mild-mannered lady. She was going to give Penelope a wonderful home and even better than that, it turned out that she lives just one block from my office so I would see Penelope regularly!

The day after the event Penelope and Mirella came by to say hello and to tell me that Penelope was now Sienna, a pretty name for a pretty girl. I see Sienna and Mirella quite frequently, and Mirella makes a point of bringing Sienna to visit us at some of our events. I always enjoy seeing the "alumni" and how they have blossomed into confident members of a family and the community!

There was another dog that day that was my dream dog. I have always wanted a big ol' Newfoundland (Newfie). I think they are exceptionally pretty dogs, despite all the drool. As I was helping unload the dogs, there he was, my man. Jack. Jack was perfect. He was a solid black Newfie/Flat Coat Retriever mix. He was eight months old and breathtaking. I wanted to adopt him in the worst way! What a beauty. The funny thing is that I think they were calling him Blackie, and the guy who adopted him named him Jack. Jack is exactly what I would have named him. He just looked like a Jack.

I spent at least two hours holding on to Jack. He had been neutered the day before so he wasn't feeling his best. We sat on the floor together, and I told him how handsome he was and how lucky someone was going to be to get such a gorgeous pup. My volunteer Karen is also a lover of the *big* dog, just like me. She fell in love with him and immediately called her friend Steve. Steve came by, took one look and fell in love. I was thrilled because at least I knew someone who knew the new owner, and now I would be able to keep tabs on him to see how he made out.

Jack turned out to be an extremely mellow dog. Steve brings him by to most of the events to say hello. It is wonderful to see how well he is doing and how much he has filled out. I took so many pictures of him that day that he ended up in one of the newspaper articles that were written about the event.

One of the other more memorable but less happy stories from that day featured Muzzie. Muzzie was a great big Cane Corso. He was brindle in color and extremely sweet. Even though he was a big dog, he was actually about fifteen pounds underweight. No one would give Muzzie the time of day because of his size. He had been in the shelter for so long that this was his last event; if he didn't get a home by the end of the day, his time was up. We made certain to tell as many people as possible that very important piece of information in hopes that perhaps he would be a mercy adoption. But, much to our disappointment, there were no takers.

About one hour before the end of our event one of the kids from the church who was volunteering decided to adopt Muzzie. I was not thrilled with the adoption, but beggars couldn't be choosers. It was either this kid or death. The kid's name was Joe. His mom came by, met the dog, was less than thrilled with his size and reluctantly agreed to allow Joe to adopt him. My gut told me that this was a really bad move, but I also figured that if it didn't work they would call us and give us a chance to re-home him. So with that in mind I was kind of okay with the adoption.

To make a very long sad story short and not so sad, it turned out that Muzzie jumped up on the ninety year old granny the next day and bit her. Rather than call us to let us know they didn't want him, they returned him to the shelter. When someone returns a dog to the ACC and says that it bit someone that is a very bad thing for the dog. In many cases it means euthanasia, preceded by ten days of solitary confinement. The Department of Health puts a ten day hold on the dog and then at the end it is evaluated and usually euthanized. We didn't think that was fair to Muzzie. We felt strongly that he deserved another chance. So we did what we thought was the right thing. We called the Department of Health to plead his case. The guy who was the decision maker on the case didn't want to hear anything I had to say and abruptly ended our conversation. From there I called Richard at the ACC and pled Muzzie's case. I begged him to get the Department of Health to at least allow the dog to be seriously and fairly evaluated before making the decision to kill him. If he passed all their tests, one of my volunteers was willing to adopt him. We were happy that at least he would get a chance at a second chance!

The tens days seemed to drag. I kept thinking that if these ten days felt long for me, how long they must have felt for poor Muzzie. Muzzie, in my mind, was just a misunderstood one year old pup. It wasn't his fault he didn't have manners or know his own strength. It was the fault of the owners who got him as a cute little pup and did absolutely nothing to try to ensure that he learned manners. But now who was paying the price? Not the ignorant owners, but poor, silly, goofy Muzzie. The day finally came for the evaluation. I anxiously awaited *the call*. The call came from the evaluator herself. She had tested Muzzie in four categories, and he failed them all. They had deemed him un-adoptable and were going to euthanize him. To say that I was crushed was an understatement. I asked her to please give me some time to make a few phone calls before anything happened to him. I wanted to discuss the results with Karen to see what she thought. She was the volunteer who had expressed an interest in adopting Muzzie. I knew that my Gallagher would have failed the tests they had just administered to Muzzie but that didn't make her a bad dog. Perhaps the same were true for

Muzzie. After giving Karen all the information from the behaviorist, she had to make the tough call of rescinding her offer of adopting him. She had too many other animals in her home and, if his behavior was at all aggressive, it could be a big problem. Sadly, after all of the noise we made trying to get him a reprieve, Muzzie was put to sleep anyway. I really felt like I failed the big, loveable fellow. I had spent so much time with him and the image of those beautiful, sad eyes kept me awake at night for over a week. I must say that I appreciated the courtesy we were given by the ACC with regards to Muzzie and how they handled this case. They couldn't have been any fairer. This is when this kind of work becomes tough . . . when we lie awake with such awfully sad images of these animals in our heads all night!

NUGGIE

NUGGIE IS OUR puppy. Although she is not a puppy anymore, we still call her our puppy. She is three years old and has been in the terrible two's for over two years. Nuggie's real name is Nuggatini because when we purchased her, she was two pounds and Sal kept calling her a Nugget. She was going to be named Teddy because she looked like a little stuffed toy when we got her, but then I started calling her teeny-weenie and, between that and the whole Nugget thing with Sal, we ended up with a Nuggatini that we call Nuggie.

Nuggie is fresh and rambunctious. There is no other way to describe her. She is the most demanding little brat around, and it is our fault entirely. We have had her since she is eight weeks old. She has never experienced a moment of discipline and could be a poster child for what not to do with a pup! Nuggie is the most persistent little booger you could ever meet. At seventeen pounds, she *rules* the house. She'll torture you until she gets her point across about what it is that she wants, and she *always* wants something!

Nuggs is the one that has the one sided love-fests with the poor cats. Having been around the kitties since eight weeks old, she thinks that they are fellow dogs that just smell and bark differently. She *expects* them to play with her. Not only do they *not* want to play with her, they certainly don't want her smelly little kisses, but Nuggs doesn't care. They are getting kisses anyway, and that's that. It's hysterical to watch these love-fests with those poor guys, especially our cat Mow-Mow. Mow-Mow is huge compared to Nuggs, about eight years old and very vocal. She has kind of a sing-songy meow, thus her name. When she is the victim, we hear a very prolonged meow and, when we look to see what's going on, all we see is the big fat Mow-Mow turning her head from side to side trying to breathe because she is literally being smothered in kisses. I know all too well what these poor cats are going through because she does the same to Sal and me. When she gets in the mood for love, she will jump up onto the chair or couch we are sitting on and will literally smother us with the fastest kisses we have ever experienced. She has a long tongue and tries to clean our brains by sticking it up our noses as far as she can. Not only is it disgusting, we can't push this little freak off us. She becomes like a super-hero and is *so* determined and so strong. When we are finally able to get her off us and we try to catch our breath for a few seconds, with the blink of the eye she's back starting her love-fest all over again. This is just one of the many times when it becomes apparent that she doesn't know any commands; but then again, how can we discipline a little ball of fluff trying to smother us with love without risking hurting her feelings? We can't! So we don't even try.

I know I said that we bought her. While I am vehemently opposed to buying animals, Nuggie was a mercy-buy. She was in a pet shop and looked like she was going to die. She was this tiny, adorable little thing, shaking from the cold. It was a freezing December day and the showcase that Nuggie was in had no heat because the store was newly opened and the heat was not working. Poor Nuggie had a cold and had boogers coming from her nose. She looked pathetic. Nuggs was a tiny, frail and shivering little thing. Sal and I had gone in there just to "look." We needed a leash for Monster but walked out with an $800 mutt, pee pads, a pee pad holder, puppy food, one bottle of disgusting smelling stuff that smells like poop to spray on the pee pads and is supposed to give the pup "the idea," a tiny harness, a few puppy toys, a puppy playpen and an enormous new charge to my credit card.

This was probably one of the craziest things I have ever done. I needed a third dog like I needed a splinter in my eye. Nuggs was beyond adorable, but what a royal pain. I have sworn off puppies since I got her. I'd forgotten how difficult it was to house-train a pup, and it took us eighteen very long months to get her to finally do everything outdoors, all the time. Thank goodness she is little and little dogs take little pees, but still, cleaning up pee gets real old after the first month, and eighteen months into it we just started wondering what is *wrong* with the little mutt—why can't she get this simple concept?

When we first got her, Nuggie was smaller than any stuffed animal we had ever seen. At eight weeks and less than two pounds, she was the size of a beanie baby, small and very cute. Much to our surprise and disappointment, Monster was terrified of her. For the first four months he'd run away and hide from her. He didn't like her one bit. Sal and I felt awful about this because we thought that they would be best of buddies. Gallagher on the other hand thought she was cute, but not when she decided to do "the Mommy Dance." The Mommy Dance is adorable—what it equates to is a belly dance done on Gallagher's nose—picture it—Gallagher is lying down on the floor with her face in between her front paws. Nuggie will go over to Gallagher and wag her little booty like crazy, then she will inch her way closer and closer to Gallagher's big nose and will gently put her back leg up on Gallagher's nose so that her little belly is almost touching Gallagher's nose. Once in this position, she will wag her little cropped-tail so fast that we can hardly see it, all the while keeping her little back paw on Gallie's nose. We call this the "Mommy Dance"! This little rendition goes on for about a full minute before Gallagher starts to let out a low growl to warn her that the song's over!

Nuggie loves to "dance" and does a very funny "toy dance" as well. The toy dance plays out like this . . . She grabs one of her toys and like she was shot from a gun will come running over to show us her toy. While showing the toy, which she has in her little mouth with all her long, flowing fur hiding it, she is "dancing" and puffing out air. Her favorite time to do this is when I am lying down on my back on the couch. She dances all over my chest with her silly toy, and we say, "Nice toy, Nuggie, nice toy." The more we say this, the more excited she gets. The longer she dances, the faster the dance becomes—we cannot believe how much one little booty can shake and how fast a little nub can wag.

Nuggie also does the "nice" position. When Nuggie is being fresh and we raise our voice to her, she will do "nice." "Nice" is her stretching her front paws out in front of her and putting her little booty up in the air, I think this is the Downward Dog pose in yoga, but I'm not sure. When she does this, no matter how fresh she has been, we always say, "Nice Nuggie, nice, good girl . . ." so, when she knows she is being bad and feels sad about getting yelled at, she will do "nice," and "nice" makes everyone forget about what was going on in the first place.

Nuggie has many nicknames, just like Gallagher. One of the ones she responds to without hesitation is "Wormy." I started calling her Wormy because of the way she wiggles her body when she is happy. She looks like a wiggly worm. Another nickname for her is Buggy. Whenever we pick her up, which is all the time, we always say, "One, two, three . . . Up the Buggy!" She is so conditioned to this that by "three" her feet are off the ground and she is ready for lift-off. One of the reasons that we have to pick her up so much is that she refuses to walk down steps. Doesn't matter what is at the bottom or how badly she wants to get to the bottom, she will not even attempt to go down. We're actually okay with this because sometimes when we are trying to get all three dogs out for a walk, it gets hairy, and we worry that one will run down the stairs and get away. So with Nuggie being afraid it is one less to worry about; it works out well.

Nuggs makes the wildest sounds when she wants something and doesn't stop making those sounds until she gets exactly what she wants. The only way to describe the sound is that she sounds like a burro. So we call her Burro-Buggie when she starts on one of her tirades. These episodes are usually food or toy-related, and once she finally gets us to understand whether it's a cookie, wet food, dry food or a squeaky toy that she wants, she will finally stop. But not until her point is made!

Nuggie has food issues which we completely attribute to Monster being a thief. When Nuggs was a pup, the moment she would turn her head away from her food, Monster would do his suction cup impersonation and eat it all. As she got bigger, she got braver and developed a wicked growl. The growl seems to work as long as she is sitting within lunging distance of her food, otherwise the little dude is quick to work his magical disappearing act. Because of this, Nuggs has issues with eating and food. We feed all three dogs at the same time, but Nuggs chooses to guard her food rather than eat it. She likes to antagonize Monster by waiting for the right moment to eat, which usually takes hours. She will guard the food like crazy. Any other animal that even glances in that direction is greeted with this deep, vicious sounding low growl. Gallagher, for the most part doesn't challenge her. Monster, on the other hand, still tries to sneak some. The poor cats have absolutely no idea why they are getting growled at when they try to walk past the dish. They look at her as if to say that they have no interest in a plate of dog food and that they're high class cats with discriminating taste buds.

Nuggs is full of strange habits, but her funniest is her "sobriety walk." When we are out on our walks with her and the other guys, we can always tell when she's getting ready to poop. She doesn't go in a circle like some dogs, she doesn't walk to the curb like other dogs. No, Nuggs walks the straight lines in the sidewalk, as though she were at a DWI checkpoint. She does this for at least three or four houses and *then* she squats and poops. But if the line is crooked it throws her off, and she has to start the walk all over again. It is the strangest thing we've ever seen, and she does this all the time. Sal and I, being the goofy pet owners we are, just add this to the long list of other things that she does that we think are just "too cute."

PATCHES

PATCHES WAS ADOPTED out in February 2005 at our "Lovey Dovey Adoption Event." She was a very timid, nervous and sad dog. Her papers said she that she was an owner-surrender because they were moving, and that she was a beagle mix, but I didn't see it. To me it was very difficult to say what she had in her. She was not outwardly beautiful, and because at five years old she was close to middle age, she was not a dog that was getting a whole lot of attention. This made her even more endearing to my volunteers. Everyone felt so sorry for her. She certainly was not enjoying being in the center of so much activity. We could see from her down-turned ears and tail tucked under her belly that she was extremely nervous. The more I watched her, the sorrier I felt for her. What she needed was a quiet, peaceful place to call home. Fortunately, at this adoption day we did advertise it as a Senior for Senior event because we were anticipating having older dogs like Patches involved in our day. Now, the challenge was connecting the right Senior with our distressed little lady!

About three hours into the day, a lovely older man named Mr. Hansel came in. He immediately took to Patches. He spent some time petting her and talking to her. Trying very hard to get her to trust him, he sat down in a chair and spoke very softly to her. Eventually, her face and body seemed to relax a little, and her tail even had a low, slow wag to it. She was warming up to him. My parents had been visiting the event that day, and had gotten a soft spot for Patches. As they watched this love-fest begin between Patches and the older gentleman, my mother had tears running down her face. She was so happy to see that someone had finally expressed an interest in this sad, overwhelmed pooch. After chatting with Mr. Hansel for a few moments, he took out his wallet to show me the love of his life . . . his sixteen year old dog that had recently passed away. His eyes filled with tears just talking about her. He went on to say how much he missed her and how lonesome the house was without her. I could completely identify with him and tears filled my eyes as we shared the grief that only pet owners who have lost their wonderful pets can share. Until someone has had a pet die on them, they can only imagine how awful it is, but to experience it is something so completely different. And then, we meet the people who have never been lucky enough to know what it is to love and be loved by a pet. They just don't get us, and say things like, "It's just an animal . . ." not having any clue how insensitive that one sentence is to people like us.

Mr. Hansel decided that Patches would be his new lady-friend. He happily proceeded to the Adoption Processing Table and filled out the paperwork. Everyone was so excited to see that Patches was getting a chance at a nice quiet life! We had really been worried about her and the possibility that she wouldn't get adopted. Being she was so overwhelmed at all the activity going on, she wasn't confident and wasn't showing as a dynamic dog, but rather as a very mousy, overly timid pet who might be difficult to have around. We were all concerned that this would be working against her, and to send a dog like this back to a shelter and that environment would be devastating to both the dog and to us!

Once all the paperwork was completed, Patches seemed to understand what was going on. Her tail, for the first time all day, was raised high and her eyes seemed bigger and brighter! As she and her new owner strolled out the door, I felt tears roll down my cheeks. This was a perfect match. She needed a kind soul, and he needed a warm, furry, calm friend. Things were good.

Eight months passed, and I didn't hear anything about Patches. I like to believe that No News is Good News. So, I was quite disturbed when I received a call from a woman named Julia. She had been referred to me by one of the vets that I deal with. It turned out that her dad was very sick with heart problems and was in the hospital. The dad had a dog, and she needed to find someone to take the dog. As it was, the dog was by itself in the house all day, and she and her husband were passing by to feed it. I know that what I am going to say may not be fair, but this made me mad. I asked Julia if she had a dog of her own, and she said no. I then asked her why she doesn't take it to her house rather than have the poor dog feel abandoned in the empty house. I got a very unemotional, empty response with no explanation offered—just "No, I can't do that." From this small snippet I sensed that Julia was no animal lover and that I had better make sure that I help out with the dog or who knows what might have happened to her.

I told her to find out how old the dog was, if it's been fixed, up to date on shots, what kind of dog and whether or not it is good with kids and other pets. Reluctantly, she agreed. I suggested that she call her vet to find out answers to most of the questions I asked her. The next day, I got a call from her saying that she had found the paperwork on the dog in the father's house. She was a five year old Beagle mix and she was fixed. I then asked her how long her dad had had the dog for. She said, not long, only since Feb. Then it hit me . . . I knew who this dog was . . . Oh no . . . I asked her the dreaded question, "What's the dog's name?"

"Patches" she said. Immediately my heart sank.

I said to her, "Your dad is Mr. Hansel?"

She said yes, and asked how I knew. I explained to her that I was the person he adopted Patches from. It was a small world that she would end up calling me, of all people.

Despite only looking in his seventies, Mr. Hansel was eighty-five years old. Now, he was in the hospital, very sick, and asked that the dog be found a new home. I felt so sad but agreed to help. I felt that I had a responsibility to both the man and the dog to make certain that there was once again a happy ending. I promised the daughter that I'd work my magic and call her in a few days. Sure enough, within three days, I had found a wonderful girl to take Patches. She was looking for a dog that had all the characteristics of Patches; calm, housebroken, friendly, good with kids and fixed. We arranged to meet at Mr. Hansel's home the next day.

Upon arrival, Mr. Hansel's grandson was sitting on the couch with Patches lying up against him. We could see that the dog loved this kid so much. Once again, Patches was nervous because of all the new faces, and was trying to attach her whole body to this kid. She was so sad looking, almost as if she knew something was about to change dramatically in her world! Patches seemed to understand that we were there to take her away. Her actions made us feel that she was anxious and trying to plead with us for understanding by lying on her back and showing her belly. The girl who was going to take Patches was there along with her three year old son. The little boy loved the dog instantly! We spent a little time with the dog on the couch and then decided it was time to take Patches to her new home. Patches was afraid to leave. Her little tail was once again between her legs, and she had that frightened look back in her eyes. To comfort her we all tried to speak softly and soothingly to her as we walked outside.

My car was parked way down the street, and I was worried that she would not walk down the block for us. Julia and her family sensed that I was concerned and offered to walk Patches down the street with us. When it was time to say their goodbyes, there wasn't a dry eye anywhere. We all stood there crying; it was the end for Patches and Mr. Hansel and his family, and possibly the beginning of the Hansel family having to say goodbye to Mr. Hansel himself. Without verbalizing this, we were all filled with sadness at that possibility. Then, much to our surprise, Patches jumped into the back seat of the car and settled in easily. I felt like I could finally breathe. I hadn't realized it, but I had been holding my breath about whether or not this was going to be a big scene trying to get this sad dog into the back of my car. If she had stood back there hyperventilating and unhappy, it would have made this an even more emotional moment. I drove Patches and her new family home. Patches seemed cautious, but happy with them. She loved the little boy, and the little boy kept saying in the car how happy he was that he had a new pal. I thought that was priceless. This little boy seemed like a very compassionate, kind and gentle child, and I had no concerns of him being mean or insensitive to Patches. I am very glad to say that Patches is adjusting nicely to her new home and enjoys sleeping in the middle of the bed at night! Good for you Patches! I am glad that things worked out for you, you deserve a wonderful life!

OCTOBER 2, 2005

The Adoption Event at the Third Avenue Fair

OUR HEADS WERE still spinning from the event we had just finished, and we found ourselves planning another one. Third Avenue in Bay Ridge is a prime area. It has a New York City feel, yet, a small town feel, at the same time. We have Starbucks, Haagen Daz, an old fashioned cupcake shop, bookstores, Italian pastry shops, Italian delis, antique shops, every kind of ethnic restaurant one could want, lots of banks and real estate offices, a quaint little church and of course, bars. You never need to leave Bay Ridge, we have it all.

Each year during the first weekend of October we have a street festival on Third Avenue. The festival runs for about two miles and is attended by thousands of people. Most years the weather is perfect. When I thought about hosting an event at the festival I figured I would host it in front of my office, because I was toward the end of the festival route and I didn't think that there would be too many street noises like bands or loud kiddie rides close to my office that could upset the pets. I made up thousands of fliers. We posted them everywhere. Then, just days before the event, during a casual conversation with the new owner of the pizzeria next door to my office, I found out that he had hired a DJ to play in front of his shop. I was crushed! A DJ, with those boom-ing speakers and the noise they generate would terrify my pets. What to do now?

HSBC owns a bank just one block over from my office, and they have a huge recessed parking lot there. If only I could get them to consider allowing us to rent or use the space. I had no idea if they had anything planned for the lot or if another group had already booked it from them. It took a lot for me to get up the courage to go into the bank to approach them about using the lot. If they said no, I was in trouble! But when I finally to up my nerve, I was pleasantly surprised. They were more than willing to accommodate us. The only stipulation was that we had to leave the parking lot clean when we were done. No problem!

I came back to my office feeling like the weight of the world had been lifted off my shoulders. I could breathe easy now knowing that my animals wouldn't be spooked by loud noises. Things were looking up.

The weather was forecasted to be perfect, so that was a good thing too, as we had no indoor space in case of rain. I made a couple hundred more fliers with the new location and put them out all around the area. I got the local merchants to agree to post our signs in their window, and it looked like everything was falling into place perfectly.

The fliers that my nephew made for this event were the best yet. They were so cute, with a blue dog driving a bus. It was very funny and eye-catching. We worked very hard soliciting raffles for this event, hoping that with the large turnout we were expecting that we could raise some much needed money to help fund our efforts and to help with the cost of taking in the strays that get dumped on us. As usual there are always the store owners who gladly give, like the wonderful owner of Lavender Blue, Kelly. Kelly is a die-hard animal lover and has given a basket to every single one of our raffles. As a matter of fact, Kelly approached me about donating to us!

The morning of the event was like any other event morning, filled with a million last minute things to do. We had to meet Todd, the groundskeeper from the church, that morning. Todd had agreed to allow us to borrow some tables and chairs for the day and we were so grateful. But we had to get the stuff early because they were going to be closing down the street to traffic early and we had to get the tables to the parking lot before the street closings. Sal and I picked up all the stuff from Todd and proceeded to the parking lot. Pat was doing the coffee, bagels and balloons. When we got to the parking lot our friend Leonard was there waiting to help. Leonard had adopted a cat from us and was now on-board as someone who generously contributed to our cause, in both money and time. He cheerfully helped Sal and me open the tables and set up the chairs.

Next it was time for tablecloths and all the things we do to transform plain into festive. Since it was almost Halloween we had decorations that depicted dogs dressed in Halloween costumes. They were really cute. We used pipe cleaners to fasten the decorations to the fence around the parking lot. Then we tied balloons on the fence as well. We needed to make certain that we attracted as much attention to ourselves as possible. After all, the parking lot was a bit recessed, and if we didn't make the fence showy, we could easily be overlooked. We set up our raffle table in the street. Another volunteer named Susan manned the table all day. The sun was super strong that day. Poor Susan sat in the direct sunlight for hours selling raffles without one complaint! What a good sport and what great results she got us!

My volunteers showed up in the best of spirits. The weather was perfect, the environment was perfect, and hopefully the day would be perfect. The bus and van showed up as scheduled. Luckily we had developed such a following that we had more than enough volunteers to unload all the dogs from the bus. There is no worse feeling than not having enough volunteers to take all the dogs off the bus. Ideally, we need to have three or four to man the bus and work with the cats and then one volunteer per dog. If we are short, then some of the dogs are left in their cages on the bus. They cry, screech and beg for the chance to be shown off and considered for adoption. They seem to understand how the process works! As the dogs were being unloaded, I noticed that we had plenty of Pit Bulls. That could go either way for us. Sometimes we have great success in placing them and sometimes we have none. How would today go? Two of them looked like twins. They were both solid white and breathtakingly beautiful. Gladly, both of them got adopted. We also had a few visitors from the previous week that had been returned to the shelter—an American Bulldog named Max and the out-of-control Roxy. Roxy was still bouncing off the walls, just as she had been the week before!

As the dogs were being off-loaded my phone rang. It was a Hispanic girl named Anna. She had called me earlier in the week telling me that she had three kittens that she needed homes for and could I help her. Sure, why not. Kittens go fast, so it probably wouldn't be a problem getting them into new homes. Now she was calling to say she would be dropping the kittens off in a few minutes. I told her no problem, come on over. Sure enough, she showed up a few moments later with three very sickly looking kittens. They had bad head colds and looked skinny to me. I agreed to keep them for the day at the event and told her to call me towards the end of the day and I would let her know if they had homes or not. Thank goodness they all got homes. I was thrilled because I didn't want to get stuck fostering more kittens! When Anna called and I shared the good news with her I could hear the relief in her voice. Her landlord had been on her back to get rid of the kittens, and it was very important to her that the little guys got homes.

We had a little excitement during the event. Another dog named Max, a very hyper Fox Terrier, jumped on his handler and scratched the back of his leg. It bled a little and looked sore, but it wasn't anything that required serious first aid. We had one of our volunteers who is an EMT clean it and bandage it, and he was good as new. Initially we thought it was a dog bite, however, upon further inspection and according to eye-witness accounts it was a scratch. But before all the facts were in, one of the ACC workers banished poor Max to the bus. Max was very angry that he was being punished for something he didn't do, and he made certain to let everyone within a half-mile radius know. I couldn't bear to hear his cries. There are two things in life I have a hard time listening to, a baby crying and a dog in distress. I had to make it stop. I went on the bus, got poor little misunderstood Max out and had one of my volunteers keep him separated from the other dogs until we knew the real story. Max, although small and cute, had issues and was not adopted that day. He didn't do anything to help his cause. He was constantly barking, lunging and just generally a fresh little fellow all day. There was no getting through to him. Many people took an interest in him but after a few moments of observing him in action, they stepped away. Sad but true, Max was not considered a good match for anyone. For once I had to agree, he would have been a tremendous challenge requiring intense training. If someone had the time, energy and experience to deal with that great, but most people are just too busy these days.

We had two Taco Bell dogs that day, and luckily they were both adopted. As is usually the case with those dogs, both were timid and skittish. But because they are tiny dogs they are considered desirable. I am not a big fan of those little kinds of dogs and much prefer a big old Newfie over something like that; but as I see and hear over and over, many people feel the opposite way from me and want the "smalldog."

Roxy, the super hyper dog from our previous event, did get adopted. We were all so very happy for her because we knew her time was limited, and we would have hated to see anything happen to her just because she was ill-mannered. That wasn't her fault. She was the product of very bad owners, and they were really the ones to blame. The poor dog didn't know any basic commands or anything. A mother, son and daughter team adopted her that day. Unfortunately her story does not have a happy ending with this particular family. Ultimately it does end happily, but it takes re-homing her one more time.

Max, the-oh-so-good-looking American Bulldog was adopted by a couple proclaiming themselves to be big-time animal lovers. When I looked at them, my gut told me that they weren't the right fit, but for some reason Max really responded to the man. The woman said she was a vet tech, knew so much about dogs and swore that they would give Max a great home. Max left the parking lot happily jumping up and pulling on his leash. I could see that he really liked his new owners, and I hoped that they liked him just as much. It wasn't until the end of the week that I heard from Latisha, the Off-site Event Coordinator for the ACC, that the guy had called and said that he was bringing Max back to the shelter, by subway no less, because Max was not a purebred dog and because he had chased the cat. That didn't sound like big-time animal lovers to me. Once again I knew I should have gone with my gut and discouraged this adoption. Poor Max must have been so disappointed.

Overall, our day was terrific. It wasn't until we sat down to dinner after the event that Pat and I realized how completely physically exhausted we were. We never realize how tired we are getting during the events because we run on excitement, but at the end of the day, boy do we feel it. Despite exhaustion our spirits were high having only sent back one dog, Max, the little terror, and even that made us feel bad. There had to be someone that could handle that little bundle of energy and nerves without losing their cool. We hoped that that person would find him in the coming week at the shelter. In situations like this, I don't inquire about the fate of the dog because sometimes the answer is just too painful, and I am better off wondering than actually knowing. That's how I left it with Max.

FALL 2005

Chuckie

A T THE TIME I didn't know Chuckie's name. I just knew him as the big, beautiful black Lab with a little white on his snout that the tall lady used to walk. That's all I knew about him. From across the street he would always give Sal and I and our dogs a special little hop and a big bark to greet us. Because he was a large, neutered male, I knew that we could not go over and make friends with him because Gallagher has no use for large neutered males and shows her Alpha side if she gets within ten feet of them. So with this in mind, we always kept our distance. Chuckie's owner was a woman named Maryann. She was tall, somewhat large sized with very short black hair. She appeared to be a sad, lonely woman who immediately lit up when we said hello to her. She always admired our dogs from a distance. Maryann seemed to be a big animal lover like ourselves and we could tell that she was crazy about her best friend and constant companion, Chuckie. I would see her walking all around the neighborhood with Chuckie; as a team they covered a lot of ground.

The thing that stood out the most about them was that 99% of the time she walked him in the street. It is important to understand why this is odd in our neighborhood; Bay Ridge is a busy area, and many drivers disobey the traffic laws. The streets have many cars being driven by young punks driving too fast, foreign car service drivers driving like they have no knowledge of our traffic laws, or some seniors who shouldn't be driving any more. I would not walk my dogs in the street and am actually a little nervous when I have to cross the streets with them. I worry that I may not be able to get Gallagher to move quick enough, and even though the law says the pedestrian has the right of way, in Brooklyn at times, it seems that many of the drivers don't seem to know about this law.

It was October of 2005, and we had been having a tremendous amount of rain for almost a week. Having opened up my own real estate office six months before, I had been working seven days a week and was low on energy. This one morning I decided to ask Sal to open the office at 10:00 a.m. for me so I could take my time getting Screamin Mimi, a tiny black kitten I was fostering, ready to come to work with me. It takes time to heat up the water, put it in a thermos, get her bottles ready and then pack her up and leave. So, I welcomed the chance to have Sal give me a break. As I was warming a bottle for Screamin Mimi, the phone rang, and it was Sal. A woman Kathy that I knew from the neighborhood had called. She said that her friend was killed walking her black Lab during the night and that the police had taken the dog and she wanted my help in finding out where the dog was. Instantly, a shiver ran down my spine. I knew who it was without even hearing any more information. It was Chuckie's mommy. I called Kathy to confirm what I already knew. Poor Maryann, poor Chuckie. What a tragedy. This was awful. As the rain continued to drench us, it reflected the mood of all of Maryann's friends, distraught.

I began to make my round of calls. It turned out that poor old Chuckie was turned over to the shelter that I do volunteer work with—the ACC. At any age he didn't belong there, but being the ripe old age of eight, Chuckie certainly didn't belong. Imagine what was going through his head as he sat in a cold, unfamiliar cage in a shelter. He must have been so confused, especially after what he had just been through. The initial rumor was that Maryann's family didn't want the dog. Then we heard that the family decided that they did want the dog. All I knew was that Maryann would be heartbroken if she knew her beloved Chuckie was sitting in a stainless steel cage in a shelter. It killed me to think of it. He must have been so sad. I finally got a chance to talk to my connection at the shelter. As we spoke Maryann's sister called and said she would take the dog, but not until after her sister was buried—two days from then. Poor Chuckie, those two days were going to seem like an eternity for him. He went from being Chuckie the most walked dog in Bay Ridge, to Chuckie, a big old caged animal with no one to console him on his tragic loss.

In the meantime, I had tried to get in touch with a Lab rescue group to see if they knew which one Chuckie had been adopted from. If the sister did not want the dog, then the dog should go back to the rescue group it came from to be placed, unless, of course, I could place him in the meantime. So I had left messages with a few places, and I had also spoken with my other animal loving friends about the situation. It was incredible how many people knew Maryann, didn't know her name, but knew Chuckie's name! Everyone was heartbroken by the news and all shared my concern for Chuckie's well-being. I then began to get calls from people willing to take Chuckie. They all felt like they owed it to Maryann to take the dog, even though none of them knew her name, just the dog's. So many pet owners can identify with this: knowing the dog's name but hardly ever remembering the owner's. I felt so encouraged by the good will of all of my fellow animal lovers in the community. It was wonderful to see how people rallied around an animal that had just been through a terrible, traumatic experience. It kind of makes me forget that I am in the big city.

In the meantime, the local paper published an article about Maryann, and even they didn't have her name! They did, however, have two of the most heartbreaking pictures of Chuckie standing with his big beautiful tail straight down, at the accident scene with three police officers petting his head. What was this poor pooch thinking? He for sure understood that something terrible had happened. I got so choked up at this thought. The writer did not know when he wrote the article that Maryann had been killed. Instead he described her as critically injured. But the truth was she was dead. Then the article went on to say how Chuckie remained by Maryann's side until she was taken away in the ambulance. Chuckie was a loyal friend to Maryann to the very end. Chuckie could have been spooked by the noise and the chaos that ensued and ran away, but instead he assumed and fulfilled his role as man's best friend and stayed by Maryann's side until he was no longer allowed. It doesn't get much more loyal than that. God bless Chuckie; I hope that wherever he ends up that he is treated with the respect and dignity that he so earned and deserves. As for Maryann, the story goes that it was 2 a.m. and, as was her thing, she was walking in the street in the pouring rain in a black sweatshirt and the driver never saw her. Maryann, I am sorry I never got a chance to enjoy a conversation with you. Rest in peace.

FALL 2005

No Date for the Canine Costume Party? Adoption Event

OUR "No Date for the Canine Costume Party? Adoption Event" was slated to be one of the most fun filled events we had done to date. We were asked to host this event as part of another event that a local group was hosting. Their gardens are a lovely stretch of parkland that had been neglected and then taken over by this grassroots neighborhood group and transformed into the most wonderful gardens anyone could ever imagine. Located right on the water in the Bay Ridge area, the view was simply breathtaking. We could see Manhattan, Staten Island and New Jersey from this spot, and the view of the Verrazano Bridge was just awesome. Each year in late October, they host a Canine Costume Party/Harvest Festival. The outfits that some of the dogs come dressed in are hysterical. Some owners go all out for this, and what they subject their pets to on that day is a whole other story. I have seen Basset Hounds dressed as inmates, German Shepherds dressed as bride and groom, a Dachshund dressed as a hot dog—mustard and all, a Maltese dressed as an angel complete with halo, a Burmese Mountain Dog dressed as a princess and a small-breed dog dressed as a tea bag because his name was Pekoe. The list could go on and on. We were looking forward to this, and, because this is a much anticipated and talked about neighborhood happening, we had the highest expectations for this to be our biggest and best event yet.

For the two weeks leading up to the event, my volunteers and I were buzzing with anticipation and preparation. We couldn't wait to see the lines of people happily waiting to make friends with these desperate shelter pets! Unfortunately, as the date approached, the weather was going from bad to worse. It had been raining all that week, and the forecast for the weekend was not on our side. The problem was that adoption events don't have rain dates; they are when they are because shelter pets don't get second chances.

That morning, it looked as though it were going to be a disaster. Everything that could have gone wrong went wrong. Unfortunately for us, this event was one of our few purely outdoor events, and if it was to be very cold, windy or rainy, we would be doomed. Sure enough, the forecast called for severe rains and high winds for that whole weekend. Based on that information, the people coordinating the other event that we were hoping would draw us huge crowds, cancelled theirs and decided to use their rain date of the following Sunday.

When anyone called the information number for that group's event, the answering machine simply said that the event was cancelled. The promoter inadvertently neglected to say that our event was still on, so anyone calling just thought the whole day was a wash! In addition, the event promoter called the local dog groomer and gave a blanket statement to her: "The event is cancelled," but never indicated that we were still on! So the dog groomer was also spreading the word that the *events* were cancelled. To make matters worse, the person running that event went down to the site and posted signs saying the event was cancelled; again, they made *no* mention that our show *would* go on! I had gone down the day before and put up "No Parking Sunday" signs so that we would have enough spots for the bus and van to pull in. It was pouring rain, and the wind was fierce as I did this. I put the signs up with wire because I wanted to be sure that the signs did not get blown away. But because of this lack of communication between us and this other group, someone assumed that we were cancelled and pulled down all of our signs—thus leaving us with no spots! Anyone who lives in Bay Ridge knows that this is a disaster! Parking here is an ordeal. We can search for "a spot" for twenty—even thirty minutes sometimes—and we needed six *together!*

Needless to say, upon arrival this parking issue was a huge downer—cars were parked in all of our reserved spots and not even one "No Parking" sign could be found! *Stress!* We hoped that some of the cars would pull out before the bus came but, in the meantime, we had to set up. We tried to unload the cars of all the things that we usually use at these events: table cloths to dress up the tables we had lugged there, helium filled balloons, posters with pictures and captions of previous events, posters with copies of newspaper articles done about us, decorative posters, etc. With the wind blowing so fiercely, we had to pack up everything quicker than we unpacked it. We couldn't do any of the things we normally did. Right down to the nametags and the raffles—nothing would withstand the wind. Being just yards off the water, the wind was biting cold, there were clouds everywhere, and we kept getting the occasional sprinkle. It wasn't looking good for us!

I got in my car, drove to my office and made a few hundred more fliers. I then went around to all the local shops and delis and begged them to please give my fliers to anyone who shopped in their store that day. I also left some in the Starbucks, in the lobby of the Chase branch next to the ATM machines, and a few other places that I knew people might be stopping into on a Sunday afternoon. I was desperate and desperate times call for desperate measures. I even had my younger sister, Susie, going all around the town dropping off fliers at the stores and to people on the street. After I finished running around with the fliers I drove back to the shore with a heavy heart. I hate to let the pets down. We are their only chance, and it was killing me to think that we could really fail this time!

At a typical adoption day, we would have people lined up for an hour before the bus pulled up eagerly anticipating the arrival of the pets. Today, we had three people—there as a group! We were sick! So much work had gone into planning this event, and the bus and van that pulled up were both chocked full of sad, desperate faces counting on us to free them from shelter life! My volunteers and I were heartsick at the idea that this event would be a bust and most, if not all, of these innocent creatures would be sent back to the shelter. To make matters worse, most of the dogs were big and big dogs are really hard to place. The anxiety and somber mood among the volunteers was thick. We had never started the day off on such a bad note, and we could only pray that things would improve for us! "Please God," I kept saying. "You have been so wonderful to us for all the other events, don't test us now! Please, let the wind die down, the clouds disappear, and would it be asking too much for some sun?"

I always say that God is good, and once again he came through for us. Within an hour of the bus pulling up, the winds died down, the sun started to peek out and the day was becoming a reasonably nice one. By 1:00 p.m., we had ourselves a terrific day! We were not as organized as we would have liked, but that was okay. People were starting to come out. It seemed that many people didn't know that the other event had been cancelled, so we ended up having a wonderful turnout. We were lucky enough to adopt out twenty-six of the twenty-eight pets that were sent. Three of the dogs we had were slated to be euthanized the very next day, so we worked very hard to make certain that they did not go back on the bus. They were a tough sell; their names were Thomas, Belvadere and Bandit.

Thomas was a five to six year old Rotti Mix. He was a very sweet, mild mannered and slightly overweight fellow. I really liked him because he was a mellow kind of a guy and the older I get the more I like the mellow dogs. This guy was sweet in every way. He looked so sad, and, because he was just an ordinary, middle-aged, chubby guy, it didn't look good for him. We put a bright orange bandana on him to dress him up and that seemed to boost his spirit. Suddenly, he seemed happy to be there and started to shine. Within two hours, he found himself a wonderful home. He was a sweet guy just looking for love and good meals. That's not too much to ask for, and he found it in a wonderful woman. She stopped by my office the following month to say hello and to tell me how terrific "Thom-Thom" was. I asked her to please bring him by to say hello sometime! Within five minutes I had a wonderful visit from a very happy Thom-Thom and plenty of kisses! What a great dog! Another wonderful save!

Next there was Belvadere. He was an eighteen month old, energetic, extremely handsome fellow with eyes that melted my soul! Belvadere was a Lab mix and because of that, he was on the large size. Although on the thin side, he was still about seventy pounds. Seventy pounds for most people living in an apartment is considered to be "too big." This was the recurring comment for him all day. "He's beautiful, but too big." As the day passed, we were getting more and more nervous about his fate. None of the volunteers could take him because of the size and energy combo. He would be too rambunctious for anyone with timid or older pets and most of the volunteers have one or the other or both. By 3:00 p.m. we were all very tense. It wasn't looking promising for him and this would be a real heartbreaker for us. A perfectly healthy, gorgeous, young and energetic boy put to sleep for no reason other than being "too big." This was killing me. God once again was smiling on us. At 3:30 p.m. this lovely couple with a large dog of their own came by and fell in love with Belvadere. The jubilation that filled the air is beyond description. There wasn't a dry eye in the crowd. Everyone was cheering and hugging each other. These moments are precious and the feeling of camaraderie among the volunteers is so strong! This is what these events are about, placing hard to place pets and saving their lives! I have a wonderful picture of him walking off into the sunset with his new family!

And then there was Bandit. Bandit was another five-ish fellow. His story was sad. He had gotten lost, and when Animal Control scanned him they found out that he was micro-chipped and contacted his owner. The owner declined his right to pick the dog up. The dog was placed on a ten day hold in case the owner changed his mind and then put up for adoption. Bandit was a sad boy. I could see from the look in his eyes that he felt betrayed. His tail stayed low, and his demeanor was that of a defeated pooch. With his sad Sam look—shaggy, unkempt fur and flaking skin—he didn't show well. It was no surprise to us that he was not getting adopted. Most people overlook the sad, sloppy dogs. But these dogs are sad for a reason. In Bandit's case, he went from being a pet in a home to an unwanted stray whose owner betrayed him and now found himself in a very stressful shelter situation. For most of these pets, the bus ride to the event itself is a very stressful thing. When they arrive, some have themselves worked into a frenzied state and impatiently are waiting to be unloaded from those steel cages. Bandit was not one of those frenzied dogs, but rather just the saddest, most rejected looking fellow I had ever set my eyes on. Just because he wasn't showing well didn't mean that he wouldn't make a good pet.

The volunteers I have are wonderful and one of my best volunteers is a doctor named Karen. Thankfully, she took pity on him. She went home, loaded up her van with her three dogs and brought them to the event to meet Bandit. Bandit, because of his non-threatening nature, passed the inspection of her three pooches and was quickly loaded into her van and is now living in a wonderful home! Bandit was spared!

We had some excitement with a cat at this event. This husband and wife team had adopted two kitties from us. One was a little red and white one named Tiger. When the adoption paperwork was completed, the two kitties were placed in cardboard carriers and handed to the new, proud parents. These people lived a few blocks from the event but had driven there instead of walking. When they were in the car on the way home somehow Tiger managed to get out of his carrier and bolted when they opened the car door. Much to their horror, Tiger disappeared down a driveway and couldn't be found. The husband came back to the event very shaken up. He told us the story, and we were all upset. To add to insult to injury, the kitty had been neutered the previous day, was still sore from the surgery, and had a non-breakaway collar around his neck. This meant that if caught on a fence he could be strangled or if he stayed on the street as a stray, his collar would eventually eat into his neck and choke him as he grew!

I ran to my car, drove to my office and made loads of "Lost" fliers. I then had my volunteers plaster the immediate area with them. Within minutes of putting up the signs, we received a call from someone, but it turned out to be a wild goose chase. This really put a damper on the mood. The volunteers that work on the cat bus were just beside themselves! Remember, we get attached to our furry friends and take everything that happens to them—good or bad—to heart. The event was ending and there was no sign of Tiger.

The following week was one of the wettest and coldest weeks we had that fall. My sister- in-law, Judy, went down there looking for him after work, and my other volunteer Margie kept going down during the day, bringing food and a cage to see if she could find him. Margie rang bells and went down private driveways into people's backyards searching for him. My phone kept ringing with people telling me that they had found an orange and white cat and that they had taken the cat in. None of these cats that the people had taken in were Tiger, but it worked out well for those cats because they ended up getting homes! So at least something good did come from something bad. Finally after almost ten days we got the call we had hoped for. The owner's neighbor found the kitty. He was in the yard next door! He was a bit scratched up and dirty but other than that he was good. We learned from this experience. Now we make sure that all the cat boxes are very secure before we allow the new owners to take them off the bus. One lost cat is one cat too many.

All in all, the day turned out to be one of the best days we had ever had. The results far exceeded what we had thought we'd end up with at the beginning of the day! We didn't imagine that we would be sending back only two! Two is still two too many for us, but for a day that started out really bad—it wasn't so bad after all. Once again, the big guy upstairs came through for us!

FALL 2005

Kayla, a Life Too Short

BEING A REALTOR, I have "For Sale" and "Sold" signs made up periodically for homes that I am working on. Recently, I had my sign guy pass by my office to pick up his check. When he saw my window and all the pets that were for adoption, he asked me to help him find a home for his dog, Kayla. Kayla was a Bulldog, eighteen months old and super sweet. Patrick, the sign guy, had gotten divorced and had custody of the dog. Unfortunately for both of them, he had no time for her, and she spent over fourteen hours a day, every day, alone. Patrick felt very bad about this and decided that the time had come to do the right thing for Kayla.

Immediately I knew who would want Kayla: one of my volunteers, a wonderful woman named Karen. She had a heart of gold and a gift for working with animals. Karen had already taken in a fourth dog at our last adoption event. His name was Bandit and he was scheduled to be euthanized as soon as he got back to the shelter but because he reminded her so much of her dog Sheba, she couldn't let that happen. When it became apparent that no one wanted him, she took him home! He fits into her home perfectly! Karen was only too happy to go meet Patrick and Kayla, and it was love at first sight. She took Kayla home, only to find out that the dog was not housebroken—at all! Not fun when she already had four dogs, a bunch of cats and some baby squirrels that she was fostering.

After a week or so Karen wanted to get Kayla spayed but noticed that the dog urinated constantly. So before having any surgery performed, she decided to have some blood work done to check Kayla's kidneys. The results were shocking. The dog was in acute kidney failure! She came by my office on the way home from the vet, completely pale. Timothy and Lexington were in visiting, and Karen was heartbroken as she broke the news to us! The dog seemed so healthy, how could this be?

As we watched Kayla and Lexington horsing around with each other, I could feel my eyes stinging with tears. This was sad, really sad. Kayla was a beauty, a happy go lucky, sweet pup whose life so far hadn't been any fun. Now, when she finally has a chance to *live* and to have "friends" around her all day, her life was going to be cut short. My heart was breaking.

The mood went from fun and lighthearted to somber. We all felt so awful. We would never think, as we watched them play, that Kayla was dying! It seemed so unfair. She was full of puppy energy and fun. Karen said that she was going to have some x-rays and a sonogram done to confirm the results of the blood work. We all were hoping that the blood test results were wrong or belonged to some other poor dog, perhaps an older dog. Sadly, about a week later, she called to give me the grim news. Kayla's kidneys should have been about the size of two kiwis, instead they were the size of two small peanuts, and now Karen was left with the awful decision of deciding when it was "time."

I felt somewhat responsible for having Karen endure this heartbreak and enormous expense because I was the one that got her interested in Kayla to begin with, but, at the same time, I must admit that I was awfully glad that Kayla was able to experience some fun and enjoy "friends" before her time came to an end. Kayla's health continued to decline despite Karen's heroic efforts to keep her alive and comfortable. Unfortunately, within about six months Kayla had deteriorated so much that that awful decision had to be made, and she left this world peacefully one sad Sunday afternoon, taking a large piece of Karen's heart with her as she departed. Bandit had befriended Kayla, and he took her passing very hard as well. God bless you Kayla, and say hello to my Buckwheat for me. Tell him that I still miss him terribly!

FALL 2005

Sleeping With One Eye Open

IT WAS TWO days before Thanksgiving when I received a call from a desperate woman who had seen a flier for our upcoming "Paws to Give Thanks Adoption Event." She was very nervous and spoke very quickly. It seemed that she had two children, ages two and five. In October, the two year old developed asthma, and the doctor told the mom that she had to get rid of her two cats. These cats were her original babies, and she was heartsick over it. Her husband, on the other hand, was a miserable, animal-hating man who couldn't wait to get rid of them. For the past month she had been trying, unsuccessfully, to find someone to take these lovely cats from her. Now she was desperate.

The husband was threatening to open the door and kick them out at night while she slept. She was terrified of him and knew only too well what kind of a heartless creep he could be. She told me how she slept all night with one eye open and listened for the door. She was sick over this. She had gotten pneumonia and was really feeling badly and at the same time still had to contend with this jerk's threats. She was hoping that I might be able to help her find homes, as soon as possible.

I did the usual thing. I told her to send me pictures, to tell her husband to relax and to give me a little time; I would be happy to work my magic for her and her two lovely cats. The cats were seven and eight years old and had been with her their whole lives. It was going to be hard for the three of them to part ways, but she had no choice. I also told her I would try to get someone to foster them in the meantime, so that we could make sure that they stayed safe while awaiting their new home.

The adoption event was that weekend and along came a woman crying. She asked for me and was pointed in my direction. As she walked towards me, I wondered why she was crying and who she was. It was the woman who had called me about the two cats! Her situation had changed, she cried. Her husband was now beating her, and she needed to leave him, but because of the cats, she had to stay. He told her that if she left, he would either kill the cats or kick them out, and she had not doubt that he would follow through with his threat. So, jeopardizing her own safety, she continued to stay in the house with this violent bully, just to make certain that her cats didn't get killed or tossed into the street. I felt so awful. I promised her that I would try my hardest and gave her a great big hug.

Two days after this exchange, she walked into my office with her mom. She was rail thin; her eyes were swollen and red. She looked like death walking. Apparently, they had just come from filing a domestic violence report at the local police station and were really desperate for someplace to put the cats. She could go live with one of her brothers with the kids, but the cats couldn't come. Her brothers had no idea about the violence she was enduring, and if they knew they'd kill the husband, so she had to keep that part of the story from them.

She brought with her more pictures of the cats. They were beautiful cats who deserved to continue to live in the comforts of a home. Why should their lives be uncomfortable or put in danger because of this big schmuck? I spent two days searching through my notebooks, looking for anyone who might be able to foster them or adopt with no luck. Even though I had just met her, I felt for her and the pressure that she was under. Everyone I know has gotten suckered into taking in a new cat or dog from me since I started doing this "work," and I had not a single friend left that I could approach about this awful situation. What this guy was doing to her was absolutely awful—*no one* should have to sleep with one eye open!

NOVEMBER 13, 2005

You're Never Too Old to Make a New Friend Adoption Event

WHILE GETTING READY for this event we were so excited. The plan was to host a regular event with the added attraction of the Senior for Senior concept. The beauty of this was that we could have the older pets for the seniors and hopefully they would bring their family members with them to help save another pet. Kind of like a two for one event. We were certain that this would be a particularly successful day. The venue was a senior center that is run by the Parks Department of NYC. The location, while a bit off the beaten path, offered indoor space as well as outdoor space and parking. The forecast was predicting perfect weather. We thought we had it made.

As usual, we ran around posting fliers everywhere we could think of, especially libraries, churches and drug stores where more seniors might frequent. We did the usual balloons, tablecloths, raffles, posters, decorations, candy, coffee, Brooklyn bagels with all the trimmings, water, dog biscuits, dog bowls, etc. We didn't miss a thing. We arrived at the center nice and early and got everything set up in record time. We were like a well-oiled machine at this point. Everything seemed to fall into place so perfectly.

The weather could not have possibly been better. Good guy that he is, God once again was smiling on us. As 11:00 a.m. drew near I took one look around and realized we were up the creek. There were three sets of people waiting to adopt. That was it—three families. On a day like that, to only have three families show up was unimaginable. The sky was so blue, the sun shining brightly. Where was everybody? I immediately began to feel stressed. I tried to tell myself to relax, that things would pick up. That it was a Sunday and that Sunday's are different than our usual Saturdays. Take a couple of deep breaths, relax and wait for the crowds!

And so I did. I waited and waited. The crowds did not come. My volunteers, being veterans by this point, also knew that things were not good. They were getting very stressed out thinking that we were two hours into the event and we had done three adoptions. This was unheard of! As we mumbled under our breaths about how awful the turnout was and how disappointed we were with the local seniors that they didn't even come out to show support, the shelter people were doing some mumbling of their own. Finally they asked me if we could move the bus to a busier location. I immediately jumped at the chance. Two of my volunteers offered to go up to Third Avenue, right by my office, to see if the service station would allow us to have the bus pull into their driveway for a few hours. We waited on pins and needles to get the call that things were good to go. Sure enough, within five minutes we were mobilizing.

Before I could leave I had the distasteful task of apologizing to the lovely person from the senior center that had been kind enough to extend the invite to us. She was a truly kind, animal loving person, who had gone out of her way to make sure that everything was open and available to us. She even helped create the flier! I felt like two cents walking in there and telling her we were jumping ship, but I had to do what was right for the pets. So, with a very heavy heart and my tail between my legs I went inside to break the news to her. She accepted my explanation very graciously and even helped us pack up. She took it far better than I would have.

Never did balloons come down quicker or tablecloths come off faster. The posters were removed from walls with record speed. Everyone was moving like they were on fire! We posted a big note on the door saying where we had moved the event to. We ended up throwing away the coffee and bagels, but of course salvaged the chocolate. I have my priorities right. We loaded back onto the bus a bunch of very confused dogs and headed up to Third Avenue where we hoped to save the last few hours of the event!

By the time the bus pulled up to the Third Avenue location, the dogs were crazed in their cages. We could hear them barking for three blocks in any direction. This was a good thing because they were doing their own advertising that we were there but a bad thing because they make me feel so anxious when they all bark so desperately like that. Because we had moved to the new location, no one had any idea that we were there. We had to rely on foot traffic, word of mouth and a few fliers that I made up quickly in my office and had some volunteers post on poles.

We hoped that we would have some people come. We knew for sure that the results would not be our usual, impressive numbers, but every pet adopted is one less pet euthanized. In that context it's hard to feel disappointed, even with lower numbers. As usual we had terrific pets that day, mostly medium-to-large-sized dogs. The cat selection was good too, with some being a little more exotic than usual. As the time clicked away on the clock, we were so worried about what was going to happen. It would really stink to send the bus back with almost as many as it came with. We hoped and hoped that more people would hear about us being parked there and would feel the urge to come by and check us out.

At this event we had a non-shelter pooch named Max. This beautiful Papillion's owners of eleven years decided that they didn't have time for him. They had called me earlier in the week to ask if I could help re-home Max. They lived in Westchester but had heard about me and the work I do from their cousin who had a Maltese that I had helped re-home a few months before. While I hated the idea of giving away such an old dog and made a point of trying to rattle some deeply seated guilt, it wasn't happening! The owners had made their decision, and Max was not a welcome family member any more! I was so sad for him. I made countless calls before the event to try to get him a home, but had no takers. Everyone said the same thing—he's too old.

Max was the prettiest Papillion I had ever seen, with a deep auburn colored coat and a white chest and paws. He looked more like a small Collie than anything else. His owner had come by the senior center earlier in the day and dropped him off to us. The moment of abandonment was a real tear-jerker. The owner, a guy in his late thirties, got out of his car with Max and a shopping bag full of Max's belongings. Poor Max had no idea what was going on as he happily walked across the street to where the event was taking place. He politely sniffed the other dogs and was extremely well-behaved. The man spent about five minutes impatiently standing there with Max and then handed his leash to one of my volunteers and walked away. He never even said goodbye to his loyal little friend of all those years. Max watched him walk away, thinking he was coming right back. When he saw the car drive away his little tail went down, ears went back, and he looked as though he understood that he had just been dumped. The owner had a football game to get to and was pressed for time. I guess the extra minute it would have taken to give the little guy a kiss and wish him well was time he didn't have!

Sal, my husband, had watched the whole scene play out. He was crazed. He couldn't understand how someone could just betray their pet like that. He had heard the owner tell my volunteer that he had gotten the dog as a pup when he was single, but now he was married and had two kids. Max just didn't fit into their lives anymore. Sal internalized all that had taken place and was so hurt for the dog. He felt like Max understood exactly what happened, and it was breaking Sal's heart to stand there and read the dog's body language. When Sal came over to me to voice his disgust I explained to him that it was better that the dog was left off with us than taken to a shelter, which is what their plan had been. His chances of getting a home in a shelter were slim to none. How many people go to a shelter to adopt an eleven year old dog? Not many. I prayed that I would find him a loving owner before the day ended!

As the day went on, Max turned out to be the sweetest little fellow I had ever met. He was perfectly mannered, perfectly manicured and very reserved. This dog was a perfect dog. How anyone could dump him after eleven years was so upsetting. We were shocked to have the only senior that showed up for our event reject him based on his age. She, herself, was about eighty years old with a cane. Who was she to say he was too old? I guess we were all feeling a little sensitive about Max and took it a little personally that she wouldn't consider giving him a good home. As one of my volunteers was overhead saying, "He'll probably outlive her." But I felt like if she couldn't see that this boy needed an act of kindness at that moment then she wasn't worthy of reaping the rewards of having such a great little man in her life. She left empty handed, and I have to believe that she had an empty heart to begin with, so Max really didn't miss out on anything by her not taking him.

When we decided to move the event down to Third Avenue, Ruth, one of my volunteers who has never missed an event, insisted on taking Max for a walk from the senior center to the new location. She wanted to make Max feel like someone cared about him. So she chatted with him all the way from point A to point B. When they arrived Max actually looked happy, like he enjoyed his walk. Ruth took charge of Max for the rest of the day and worked very hard trying to get him the right home. That home did finally come in the form of a very kind, single woman who worked from home and needed a walking companion. Her name was Judy, and she instantly took a liking to Max. She had had a small dog like Max for sixteen years, and he had recently passed away. She was thrilled when she saw Max and didn't give a second thought to his age. Ruth was so pleased that Max was getting a good home that she took the shopping bag that contained his belongings and walked with Max and his new mommy all the way home, wishing him a wonderful life as she left. At least someone cared enough to say goodbye to the little guy and wish him well!

Another senior pet that desperately needed a home that day was Lucky. Lucky was a blind, deaf ten year old Pug. She was extremely cute and very gentle. Of course not a whole lot of people are itching to adopt a blind and deaf ten year old dog. The thing was that we didn't know the dog was blind and deaf, we just thought it was a bit old and depressed and that was why she wasn't responsive to people calling her name. When the woman who ran the senior center came by to visit our new location, she brought along her niece, an enormous animal lover.

When her niece took one look at the dog she immediately wanted it. I was shocked but thrilled at the same time. Why would a twenty-some-thing girl want such an old dog? Go figure, but she wanted Lucky. She filled out all the paperwork and held Lucky so tightly. We could see that Lucky was feeling really relaxed with her new Mommy and was quite content.

I got a call from the aunt the following week. She is the one who told me that the dog was blind and deaf. Then it all made sense. That was why the dog was very non-reactive to the other dogs, the loud noises and the people calling her name. When I heard about these two conditions, I was even more thrilled that she had a home. Imagine try-ing to adopt out a blind, deaf dog in a shelter that has lots of young, healthy, energetic pooches. I asked if the niece was disappointed when she found out the news, and she said no, that the dog was a great dog and they were enjoying her so much! See, now that's a full heart!

As for the results of that day, well, we did ten adoptions. Ten is the lowest number we have ever done, but, then again, I have to remind myself that ten adopted pets means ten less dead pets.

FALL 2005

Mike and Ike

I T WAS THE week before Thanksgiving, and my office window was chocked full of pets needing homes. I was hoping that I would have homes for everyone before the holidays, when in walked this very handsome twenty-something fellow and his dad. They were well dressed and very polite. The son was new to the area, from Missouri, and wanted to adopt a kitten from me. Since all I had were full-grown cats in the window, I told him to come to the adoption event that I was hosting that Saturday and he could pick one out.

That Saturday we were hosting "The Paws to Give Thanks" event. The turnout was not as we had hoped. We had the long holiday weekend working against us and many people were still away. Add to that all the people taking advantage of that weekend's sales, the turnout was a disappointment but not a surprise.

Towards the end of the day, the handsome fellow who had come to my office earlier in the week walked in. He seemed to be better looking than I had remembered and a bunch of my volunteers were joking about how they would have liked to have been adopted by him or that they would like to adopt him.

His name was Mark. He was twenty-eight years old and just home from the Army. He was a personal trainer and his body boasted his profession. Since we had mostly older cats from the shelter, he wasn't too interested in the animals on the bus. But inside the parish house my friend Lisa had brought two kittens that were born in her yard that she had been fostering. I told her it was fine to bring them along and that hopefully we could get them a good home. So there they were, two adorable brothers, about four months old. Both tiger striped brown and tan; one with huge eyes and the other with a rounded face. Lisa and I felt strongly that we wanted these two brothers to stay together. One was on the shy side and he needed his brother for courage. Mark took one look at them and fell in love. He adopted them both.

He had had a cat as a child, but never one of his very own. He was a little nervous and had a few questions for us. I set him up with a litter box, litter and food. I stressed to him that he needed get them to the vet for a check-up, shots, de-worming and that he had to have them fixed! He was agreeable to all of my suggestions and left very happy. Lisa was not there when he came so she never got to meet him personally. I called her after Mark left and shared the good news. Her babies finally had a place to call home.

Lisa called Mark periodically to check in on the kitties and make sure all was well. She seemed comfortable with the adoption and felt that based on her phone conversations with Mark all was working out very well. Then the call came. It was Mark calling Lisa, crying. He told her that he was suffering from severe post traumatic stress disorder and was reliving all that he had seen while serving in Afghanistan over and over in his head. The only way for him to find any relief from this constant torture was to drink a bottle of vodka a day. The vodka helped him relax and get some rest. When he wasn't drunk, his mind was constantly flashing him with terrible experiences. The main reason for the call was to tell Lisa that he was being admitted to rehab the very next morning and that he had asked the few people who had befriended him in the area if they would either watch the kitties for him while he was gone or if they would adopt them from him. No one was willing to oblige. He was heartbroken. For the past six weeks these kittens had been the only source of fun and distraction that he had. He was crazy in love with them and the thought of abandoning them was too much for Mark to handle. He couldn't bear to be responsible for them spending time in a cold cage in a shelter. Lisa told him to relax and that she would think of something.

That's when my phone rang, and she relayed to me the sad story. This perfect specimen of man should be out enjoying life and having tons of girlfriends not reliving terrible experiences from Afghanistan in his head! No one talks about all of the Marks that are now out there. I know of three from my immediate area who are all silently suffering the effects of PTS disorder from Iraq and Afghanistan. I had to help; I would do whatever it took. The least I could do was to ease his conscience and help him to go to rehab with one less awful thing on his mind! I told Lisa to give me a few minutes to think about the situation and I'd call her back.

What to do? This was a tough one. There was no time to make phone calls because he had to give them away that evening since he was scheduled to leave the next day at the crack of dawn. I wracked my brain and decided to call my neighbor and very good buddy Carole. She lived three houses down from me, and I had just sold her house and we were waiting for a closing date. Because of me and my animal antics, Carole went from having one dog to having two dogs and two cats. She and I share the same birthday, different years, but the same date and because of that we are on the same wave length when it comes to the animals. Carole's top floor apartment was vacant. We had fostered a momma cat and her five babies there the year before. So I called her and told her my dilemma and then asked her if she would mind helping me out for a week to ten days. I really didn't anticipate it taking me more time than that to re-home these little dudes. Carole being the wonderful friend that she is agreed, but under one condition—we not let on to her husband that she had the kittens upstairs. He would be furious with her! Last time she helped me with kittens she kept two of them, so he wasn't really happy with me and didn't trust that she could resist the temptation of adorable kittens. I reassured her that her secret was safe with me!

I called Lisa and told her the good news. She agreed to pass by Mark's apartment to pick up the kittens and bring them to Carole's, where I would meet her outside. Lisa called me when she was on her way over to warn me that Mark was coming along. I had mixed emotions about that. While I wanted to reassure him and let him know that I would make certain that the kitties went to a good home, I wasn't sure if I could handle what I knew was going to be a very emotional exchange. There was no choice. He was coming.

They arrived at Carole's house with the kittens inside the carrier that I had given him. The kitties looked good, but one seemed to still have a bit of a respiratory infection. Mark took them out of the carrier and held them. Then the tears began to flow. He was overwhelmed with grief. He said through his tears how much these little guys meant to him and that they were like his kids. It was killing him to say goodbye. With that, sobbing like a baby, this perfect specimen of man ran from the house. As he bolted down the steps I wanted to stop him, hug him and wish him well, but he was too fast. I yelled to him as he left the house that I would take care of the kitties and that we were all rooting for him! I don't know how much of it he heard but hoped he knew that we were genuinely concerned for him and really wanted him to get over the demons that were causing him such distress and discomfort.

After I heard the front door slam, my eyes began to fill up with tears. What a terrible shame. This young handsome fellow is now possessed by the awful images he witnessed in a country he never dreamed he would end up in. What would his future hold? Would he be able to get help and move past all that was taking up his every thought? I felt like life was so unfair to this guy. I can't stress how perfect he was. God did an excellent job when he created this guy. Everything about him was perfect—his looks, his body and his manners. He was a dream come true on the outside but had nothing but turmoil brewing on the inside.

Carole and her daughter Casey took great care of the little guys. Their names were Mike and Ike. Ike didn't seem to understand that life had changed for him once again, but Mike was all too aware. He was very nervous and wanted to hide under the radiator so that he felt safe. Carole decided to make him a cozy box to hide in. Thank goodness he took the bait and felt safe hiding in the box and gave up trying to fit under the radiator cover.

Before I sent them on their way, I wanted to take them to the vet and get them a clean bill of health. I made an appointment to bring them a few days later. On our way there, it was pouring rain and the winds were strong. Mike and Ike were little troopers through it all. Despite the cold rain being blown on them through the carrier, they never complained but rather looked around with that wonderful, wide-eyed kitten amazement. The vet weighed them and each was less than five pounds. Mike had an infection in his eye that had been neglected and caused a band of skin to grow under his eyelid. The doctor prescribed ointment for him and said that when he was being neutered she would just snip the band of skin so that the eye could open freely. Both of the guys had respiratory infections, with Ike having the worst of it. They were prescribed an antibiotic for ten days. In addition to that, I had them de-wormed and tested for FIV and Leukemia. Thank goodness both of those tests came back negative.

The fact that the dudes needed meds twice a day presented a problem with Carole continuing to foster them. How would she explain to her unsuspecting husband why she was going upstairs two or three times a day? The plan had to change, and I had to put them in my house. The only place I could keep them that they wouldn't be exposing my cats to their infection was in the hallway, so there they stayed. They enjoyed themselves so much. They used my French doors as monkey bars and took full advantage of the long length of the hallway to do laps! We would never have known that either of these little dudes was sick. They were a bundle of laughs and full of energy. I was glad to be getting a chance to spend some time with them and to enjoy their silly antics. There's nothing quite like sitting in the living room watching TV and seeing kittens through the glass on the other side of my door using it as a jungle gym. While it is amusing, it is also a little annoying because now the lovely old wood has tiny little nail marks all over it. Still, that is a small price to pay for saving two lives, and it will always remind me of them whenever I look at the door, almost like they are still with me in a way.

Within a few days I had them in a wonderful home. One of my volunteers, Ruth, met these people on her street when they were visiting their son. They had just had to put their cat to sleep and were heartbroken. Ruth suggested that they come to see me. So, sure enough they did. They really only wanted one kitty, but I told them all about the rough life that Mike and Ike had had so far and how I needed to place them together. It didn't take much arm twisting to get them to agree to them both. We agreed that they would pick them up from my office on Saturday, January 21ˢᵗ—my 43ʳᵈ birthday. It was a bittersweet moment for me. I was thrilled to see them get a good home but by the same token I hate goodbyes. One would think that after all the fostering that I have done I would be really used to that part of the game, but it is never easy to say goodbye.

NOVEMBER 26, 2005

The Paws to Give Thanks Adoption Event

PERHAPS THIS WASN'T one of the more intelligent things I've done when planning one of these events—hosting it the Saturday after Thanksgiving. It was a gamble, a very big gamble that didn't quite go the way I had hoped. While promoting this event, I was met with a lot of, "Hello? Are you nuts, it's the Saturday after Thanksgiving, and everyone will be shopping or away, what are you thinking?" My hope was that perhaps people would decide that they didn't want to shop and would prefer to come on out to our event to adopt and maybe even bring their out of town company with them! I hoped and prayed that that would be the way it went down, but much to my dismay it didn't.

Unfortunately, the best intentions sometimes don't work out! The turnout was light and although this was disappointing, it was not a surprise—just a disappointment. As usual, we had wonderful animals that day. We had a beautiful chocolate Lab/Greyhound mix named Baby and a momma Pit who had recently given birth, also named Baby. Both of these wonderful dogs were so well behaved all day. The people handling them fell in love with them because of their calm and sweet demeanor. The Lab/Greyhound mix was not adopted because she was too big, and the momma was not adopted because she had not re-gained her girlish figure after giving birth and her boobs were hanging. The people who passed these dogs over and went home empty-handed really missed out on two wonderful dogs!

Another large dog at the event was Billy, a Doberman mix. Billy's owner, for unknown reasons, had to move back into her parent's home and now had to dump the dog! This adoption event was her last chance to try to place him before taking him to the shelter. Billy was with his owner and our goal was to make sure that he got adopted! He was a very vocal, very needy, insecure pooch who craved constant attention. If surrendered to a shelter, his chances of being adopted were slim to none. His enormous size and incessant barking would be a problem. His owner, a young teacher in her thirties, was heartbroken about having to give him away and had spent the weeks leading up to the event calling me on the phone and crying her heart out. At this point, I was just as anxious as she was about getting this big, handsome fellow a good home. We had begged God to send us a family that would have someone always around to keep Billy company. I do believe that God does answer our prayers, and the answer was in the form of a perfect, big Irish family. Sadly for them, their own dog had just died, and they couldn't bear to be without a dog. There was the stay at home mom, the working dad and the five kids we had hoped for. What scenario could have been better than this? This was just the family we ordered.

Another dog from this day was CurlyQ. CurlyQ was the most bizarre looking little dog anyone had ever laid eyes on. CurlyQ had the gorgeous Newfie coat but in a brindle color. His head was the size and shape of a Newfie and his body was the same size as a Pit. He was so weird looking that he was actually adorable. CurlyQ was a stray. He had been found wandering the streets. He was a very sweet little fellow who worked very hard trying to win people over with his very calm and reserved demeanor. His coat was so soft and his big head made us just want to grab the sides of his face and smother him with kisses. Even though CurlyQ was not a big dog no one wanted him. We weren't sure why because he certainly seemed to be a perfect pet, in every way. When a dog like this doesn't get adopted I blame myself for not doing a better job promoting the event. And because this event was so poorly attended and we sent back so many, CurlyQ included, I was really beating myself up!

The two saddest dogs of the day were a six year old Cocker Spaniel named Lucky and a small mutt that was listed as a Shepherd mix but absolutely did not have anything that would lead us to believe that he was. The Cocker had the droopiest, saddest eyes and the worst ear infection I have ever "smelled." Anyone who has had a dog with infected ears knows the smell. This poor dog's ears were so bad that we could smell them from ten feet away. I almost think that the eyes were so droopy because of the pain in the ears. Anyway, poor Lucky shook his head all day long trying to get relief. He wouldn't allow anyone to touch his face or raise his ears to get a peek inside. They were hot to the touch, and it broke our hearts to not be able to give the dog some relief from his misery. Of course no one adopted him because they all saw the costs that would come with the vet bills necessary to cure this awful infection. The person handling this dog was a woman named Cathy. Cathy is a seasoned dog person, and her emotions were running high for this dog! The poor thing had little to no chance of getting a home even after being sent back to the shelter unless this infection was addressed. It was painful to imagine that the end was near for this sweet, pure-bred pooch whose bad luck began with falling into the hands of the wrong owner and then being surrendered to the shelter!

The Shepherd mix was an angry little fellow named Mike. Mike was a small dog who had many issues. He weighed a mere thirty pounds but thought he was the tough guy of the day. He didn't like any other dogs and seemed to really have it in for poor Lucky. Mike had been to hell and back. His previous owners tortured him. He had cigarette burn marks all over his body and was anxious around certain men. He was an aggressive dog, and who could blame him. Mike, with all his burn marks, didn't make a nice appearance and then when prospective adopters observed his explosive behavior, it made their decision easy. No way. Mike really made us feel sorry for him, but, in all honesty, he wasn't doing anything to help his cause. He misbehaved anytime the opportunity presented itself. My volunteer Ronnie was holding him all day. She really worked hard on his behalf! Toward the end of the day, Ronnie was coming indoors to get out of the cold for a while with Mike. Mike spotted Lucky and immediately lunged and grabbed his ear and shook his head back and forth! Lucky let out a blood-curdling screech that pierced my ears and heart. I was standing right there and saw the whole thing. Neither Cathy nor Ronnie was aware that the dogs were that close to each other so they were shocked when they realized what all the ruckus was about.

Once we got Mike to release Lucky's ear from his mouth, Lucky continued to cry for a few painful seconds and then wildly shook his head. I wanted to cry! His already inflamed ear was now even worse. I tried to look to see if Mike drew blood, but Lucky wouldn't allow me to. There was nothing I could do to make him feel better except to bend over, pet him softly and talk to him in a very soothing voice. I felt so helpless. Mike and Lucky were both sent back. Neither dog would be an easy placement.

We did have a few positive things happen at this event, one being a beautiful Collie mix named Ingrid. Ingrid was a very pretty blonde, timid and sad dog. She was about forty-five pounds and had the soft coat of a Collie and the dark snout of a Shepherd. She was extremely overwhelmed by all the noise and other dogs she was surrounded by. Her tail was down and her ears were back! I stumbled upon her and her handler in the entrance way of the church property. As I was saying hello to her I noticed that a few feet away there was a woman and her friend. The woman was crying and saying how much Ingrid looked like her dog.

As I always do, I went over to see what the tears were about and if I could help facilitate this love connection! It turned out that this was a scenario we see played out over and over at these events. The woman's dog had died in the past month, and when she laid eyes on Ingrid she couldn't believe the similarities between the two. But like many people she was battling her emotions about whether or not it is disrespectful to the dead dog to "replace it" with another dog so quickly. I do and don't understand this thought process. I don't mean to sound insensitive, but the dead pet is gone. It is gone for good and won't be back. I understand the enormous sense of grief that is experienced at the loss of a pet. I've lived it twice so far and have many more times ahead of me. However, I also feel that if you had wonderful years with your pet and you miss it so much, then why not, as a tribute to the dead dog or cat, save the life of its fellow man? Perhaps, by performing this act of kindness on behalf of your beloved friend, you may even find that your pain is not as searing. Hopefully, in a shorter time than what might have been, with the help of your new friend positively distracting you, you will be able to fondly and happily reflect back on those years you spent with that wonderful, *irreplaceable* pet.

After much emotional wrangling, Ingrid won out and was given a terrific home with this tried and true animal lover. This was a wonderful match because Ingrid was too timid for the shelter experience, and we could see that this woman would go out of her way to work wonders in building up Ingrid's confidence. This made the day a little bit better, but still the results were nowhere close to what we were accustomed to and hoping for!

FALL AND WINTER 2005

The Flier Nazi

ADVERTISING OUR EVENTS can get extremely expensive, so we resort to *illegal activities* to publicize them: posting fliers on the street light poles. We usually do about 5,000 or 6,000 fliers per event, and it takes us a lot of time, money, energy and scotch tape to pull this off. Unfortunately, there are only about four of us putting up fliers, so we have a lot of ground to cover. When the weather is nice, it's a real pleasure. But, when the winds are whipping and the temps are frigid, it can be a painful experience.

Part of my territory is Third Avenue in Bay Ridge. Third Avenue is a beautiful area that has undergone real change in the past twenty years. It is now very much like Park Slope or the Village, boasting all kinds of cool boutiques, outdoor cafés and shops. There are many upscale restaurants, lots of banks, real estate offices and other thriving businesses. The nightlife here is probably the best that Brooklyn has to offer. For these reasons, it is really important to get our fliers up on the poles in this area. We need as many people to know about our events as possible, and the foot-traffic alone is tremendous along this strip.

While posting fliers is illegal here in NYC, everyone does it. There is actually almost a space war on the poles. The moving guy has someone post fliers for him—two per pole! He is greedy. Then there are the garage sales, the Russian nannies looking for work, the woman starting an after school program for kids and the Mexicans looking for roommates. It's not easy getting space. I never like to post over someone's flier unless the date has passed and it is old news. I try to show some flier etiquette because I know how time-consuming and costly this is. Even though the flier route of advertising is the cheapest way to go, it is still not cheap. It costs about $250 per event. In addition to the cost of printing, scotch tape is not cheap, and putting up that many fliers one at a time costs a fortune in tape and time—going from pole to pole takes what seems like forever.

Despite a warning from the Department of Sanitation to stop posting fliers, we have continued because we feel very strongly that our mission is worth breaking some laws for, after all, we are not advertising a garage sale or a moving company but, rather, we are trying to save animals from being put to death. So after our first warning, we got smart. We took our contact information off the fliers. This way, it cannot be tracked to us directly to give us the ticket; which is issued *per* flier.

We were doing fine for a while. That was until the "Flier Nazi" showed up on the scene. We couldn't figure it out. Sal and I would spend hours working our way along Third Avenue from the 70s to 100th Street happily posting fliers, but, on our way back, we would see that the fliers had already been ripped off the poles. This was infuriating! What was wrong with the person doing that? Ours is a wonderful "cause." Even if he doesn't love animals, are we doing this person any harm by trying to save them? At first I took it personally. I thought that perhaps it was another realtor doing this, or a local pet shop owner. I couldn't figure it out, but I did know that my husband was itching to catch this guy in the act. I had a few choice words for him, but Sal had other plans for this guy and his hands. I tried to calm Sal down and explain that the last thing I want to spend our money on is a lawyer to defend him when he gets arrested for assaulting the Flier Nazi.

Then one day my younger sister Susie was sitting in my office and saw the Flier Nazi in action. She ran outside to get a good look at him. She described him to me perfectly. I was now on the lookout for this little creep. He was a short, baseball cap wearing fellow with jeans and a team jacket. She couldn't figure out his age but said probably in his fifties.

Then it happened. Sal and I were walking all three dogs late one evening when he decided he wanted to buy sunflower seeds. He left me outside the grocery store holding all three dogs' leashes while he ran inside. As I waited for him, out of the corner of my eye I saw the Flier Nazi in action ripping down one of my fliers from a pole across the street. Now I'm torn. Do I confront him, knowing that Sal cannot be trusted not to break his hands, or do I miss out on my chance to talk to him? I peek inside the store as he is walking across the street towards me. Sal has one person in line ahead of him; I have time for a quick exchange! So, as the little twit walked past me, my orange flier crumpled in his tiny hands, I said to him, "So, you're the guy who pulls down the fliers."

To which he says, "What, are you a professional dog walker?" What a stupid response!

So I gave him a stupid answer in a stupid voice, "Yepper, that's me, a professional dog walker." As I finished saying that, Sal walked out the door. I wouldn't dream of letting him know who the guy was, so I just told him that the guy was asking me if I was a professional dog walker because of our three dogs and then let it go. It wasn't till we were almost home that I fessed up that the guy I had spoken to was the Flier Nazi. Sal was furious that I hadn't pointed the Flier Nazi out to him. I explained that it was for his own good that I didn't because I couldn't trust him to behave himself.

As time passed, the fliers continued to be pulled down. The problem was I never could catch him red handed until one day when I was coming back from showing a house and parked at a meter across from my office on Third Avenue. As I put quarters in the meter, once again I saw from the corner of my eye, that familiar rip and crumple move. It was him! I was furious and screamed out, "Hey you! Stop that. People spend a lot of time and money to post those fliers, and they aren't hurting you!" To which his response was to walk across the street, make sure I was watching him and pull another flier off the pole as hard as he could and crumple it! I wanted to crumple him.

Another few weeks passed, and Sal and I decided that for the next event we would use thick, clear packing tape to secure the fliers to the poles, making it impossible for him to even think about pulling them down. We painstakingly went around each flier several times so that not even a tiny piece of the paper was touchable. We were certain that we were winning this battle! Let him pick on something else. As we were out on our mission one Saturday morning, there he came walking toward us with his dry cleaning in his arms. As he walked past me, we made eye contact and then he looked at the thick roll of clear packing tape that I was holding. He knew in an instance who I was. Again, I didn't let on to Sal who he was because I was certain there would be bloodshed. This guy doesn't know how lucky he is that I am cheap and don't want to waste my good money paying an attorney to defend Sal for rendering the guy's hands useless.

Our fliers were staying up with the tape treatment, and I was happy about that. It seemed as though we had won! Then one December evening, Pat and I spent three hours in the freezing, wind and cold putting fliers on the poles with the tape treatment and couldn't feel our fingers because they were so frozen. The tape was breaking from the cold and the wind was blowing our fliers all over the place. We were not having fun, but were motivated by the wonderful newspaper article that had just hit the stands about us and our upcoming event. The joy from that had given us a high, and we kept on going. After we finished, we decided to treat ourselves to a much deserved cup of coffee and a great big slice of apple spice cake with icing from the new, old-fashioned cake shop on Third Avenue. We sat down for over an hour enjoying our coffee and cake and strategizing about how we could get the word out about our events even more than we were already doing. We felt so good that we had covered so much ground and that the fliers would be up all week for people to see.

Two days later, as I walked the avenue to my office, it hit me like a brick. The Flier Nazi was back to his tricks. He had actually taken the time to pull off all of my tape and pull the flier down but left the tape in a big clump stuck to the pole, as if to send a message. I was so angry I wanted to scream. Pole after pole, he had worked his miserable fingers undoing what Pat and I had worked so hard at!

I recently had the interesting experience of confronting the Flier Nazi. It was a cold Sunday morning, and I was extremely down in the dumps. I was closing my office because the market had gotten so bad, and I was completely devastated. As I stood inside my office packing some of the very last things, I saw the Flier Nazi outside ripping a flier off the pole. Immediately, without hesitation, I walked outside. I was furious and had decided that enough was enough. I was going to have a nice little chat with this evil person. I had to do it with great calmness because my husband and brother were inside the office and I did not want Sal to have any idea who I was talking to. So, I nonchalantly walked outside and approached this demon. I stood sideways next to him with my shoulder touching his. I said in a low voice, right into his ear, "Why do you do this? Why do you pull down all the fliers? They are not hurting you!"

To which he replied, "It's illegal!"

So I sarcastically said to him, "And let me guess, you are the self-appointed flier police?"

The man was uglier up-close than I had imagined. His teeth were disgusting, his eyes were void of any kindness, and he had an all around miserable manner.

Because I was in such an emotional state, I was close to tears at all times. This time was no different. As I began to try to reason with this man that I had so much anger towards for such a long time, I began to cry. Crying works! As I cried, he became very uncomfortable and offered to make a truce with me! Imagine that—I was able to get the Flier Nazi to agree to not pull down my fliers anymore by crying as I explained to him how important my mission is and by reciting to him the ugly statistics of the local shelter. Despite the tremendous hard work and effort of the shelter staff, in 2005 more than half of the dogs surrendered had to be put down. The numbers for the cats were even more horrific!

I am so pleased that now I can go on my merry way hanging fliers on the avenue without having to re-post them multiple times! I only wish that I had confronted this man six months earlier but, then again, the tears would not have been flowing as freely and the outcome might not have been the same.

FALL AND WINTER 2005

Please, Just Send a Card . . .

S o HERE I am, it's a Friday morning in November and I'm feeling like the fattest person on earth. Over the past few years, I have managed to pack on forty pounds of fat and feel like nothing I wear can possibly hide the rolls and bulges that my body has created to hold those extra pounds. Stress . . . I am a stress eater and as any stress eater knows, stress and food go together like shoes and socks. Why am I talking about this? Good Question. It seems to me that now that I am plump, people seem to make the connection that I like to eat and because of that they have decided in lieu of sending me a thank you card or flowers, they will bring me, of all things, *cakes!*

Feeling like this makes it difficult to be gracious or enthusiastic about being the lucky recipient of these gratuities! One particular day, I was sitting in my office thinking about the fifty-seven pants and skirts in my closets that don't fit. I am not making up this number—I have fifty-seven winter weight pants and skirts that are too uncomfortable for me to even think about putting on. Tormented by this thought, I am beating myself to death emotionally about my inability to stick to a diet! So, as I am right in the middle of one of my silent tirades inside my head, there is a knock at my office door. It is Mr. Ed, an older Irish fellow who fancies his drink. Mr. Ed is a former Marine, probably sixty years ago. He came in a few weeks prior to offer to post fliers for my adoption events. I was not there, but my sister Susie thanked him so much and said that we would be very happy to have his help and that I would call him to discuss when and where I would need him to go.

A few days later, I called him, and he agreed to pick the fliers up on the day of the event and walk the avenue helping promote the animals. We never discussed money because I assumed he was volunteering; it never even crossed my mind that he would want to get paid! I just thought he was another animal lover looking for a way to be involved.

Finally the next event was upon us. There we were, freezing at the adoption event—outdoors, no shelter and literally yards from the ocean. The winds are whipping and we are getting blasted. My cell phone rings, and it is my sister. She is manning the phones in the office for me, and Mr. Ed had just come in to pick up fliers. As Susie handed him the fliers, he mentions to her that he would like to get paid off the books because he is collecting disability. Susie didn't know how to respond to this remark, so she said, "Okay, I'll let my sister know." She then calls me and tells me what just happened. Amidst all the stress that I was experiencing at that moment, I couldn't discuss this with her or make suggestions to her as to what she could have or should have said. So I tell her that I will handle it when I see him the next day.

Sure enough, the next morning, there's a knock at my office door and outside is this dejected looking older man, who reeks of booze, introducing himself to me. Mr. Ed in the flesh! He takes a seat in my reception area and tells me that he is there for his "pay." I explain to him that when I chatted with him on the phone that I just assumed that he wanted to volunteer and that it was my error; I should have made it clear to him that no one got paid for helping out and that we were all just a group of animal loving volunteers. I then asked him how much he wanted for his day's work. He said he'd "settle for a $20." So, out of my pocket flew some more money. What could I do? He looked to me like he needed this $20 more than I did, so what's a little more charity? We chatted for a few minutes and then he went on his merry way.

A few days had passed when he arrived at my office door again. He knocks on the door and asks me if I will be in the office for another twenty minutes or so. I tell him that in twenty minutes exactly, I would be running to show a property. He says okay and that he'll be back in a flash. Sure enough, he's back ten minutes later. This time he's kicking the door with his foot and pushing against it because his hands are full. In his hands he had two shopping bags—one with four cups of regular coffee and the other with an enormous Strawberry Shortcake from the best bakery in the area. I needed to eat this cake like I needed a roach crawling in my ear.

Mr. Ed explains to me that he knew he shouldn't have taken that $20 from me, but that he was "flat broke" that day and needed it, so he had no choice. But, being a kind-hearted fellow, his conscience was eating away at him. This was his way of compensating me and easing his conscience. Personally, I would have preferred he kept the money or gave me back the $20. The very last thing someone forty pounds overweight and with a sweet tooth the size of a silver dollar needs is a fresh, creamy, mouth-watering Strawberry Shortcake! Adding insult to injury, I couldn't even enjoy the coffee. It was regular, and I have a "funny" heart so I can only drink decaf. I immediately promised myself that I would give away the cake and the coffee to someone else, which I did. But, still I managed to get a healthy slice of it because I gave it to my parents, and Dad couldn't wait to open it and have a slice for himself—he cuts huge slices—so I had what was probably two slices.

Then, we move on to the following Monday. I had once again made a promise to myself that I would start a diet that morning and that I would be thin by my birthday, eleven weeks away. At 10:00 a.m. my phone rang. It was a Russian woman named Yelena. She had come into the office a week before and told me about five kittens she was working on socializing in the backyard of where she worked. She desperately wanted to find them homes before they got too big and before the bad winter weather came. I promised her that I would try to steer some people her way and hopefully we could work something out for these babies. Sure enough, I was able to get two of her kitties homes, and she was calling to express her gratitude to me. She then asked if I would be in the office for a while. I said I would be in all day. Not more than an hour later, her very pretty mom came in with a delicious chocolate cake from a Russian Bakery—chocolate and cake, my two greatest weaknesses. As I tried to look happy about the goodies, my tight waistband brought me back to reality and screamed, *don't open the box!*

Once again, I find myself facing a dilemma. As the day passed and the cake called out to me louder and louder, I found myself stressing. Imagine that, stressing over a chocolate cake. I couldn't possibly take it to my parents again. It was bad enough that I gave them the cake on Friday. Dad is a diabetic in denial, so he would eat the whole thing. I wouldn't be seeing anyone else I knew who wasn't on a diet. So, I did something I have never done in my life. I placed it in the garbage can on the corner on my way home from the office. I knew that by placing it in that particular garbage can that one of the "regular homeless people" would end up getting it. The homeless certainly needed it much more than I did. I felt almost as though it were an act of charity, as well as a much needed demonstration of my ability to practice will-power and self-control.

The month of November passed, and I still was not able to stick to a diet. Then came December and I was still berating myself for not losing any weight. What can I say? Stress was killing any possibility of sticking to a diet. With opening a new business and not being able to recruit any full-time agents, having a husband who was trying to make a career change for almost a year, and the anxiety that comes with not having a steady paycheck from either myself or Sal anymore, stress was definitely getting the better of me. Then the phone rang the week of Christmas, and once again it was Yelena. She wanted to express her gratitude to me for all the wonderful things I do for all the animals. We exchanged pleasantries on the phone and wished each other the best for the New Year. I thought we were done. A few minutes later there's a knock at my office door. It is Yelena's beautiful mom once again. She has another cake for me from her daughter. She says she wanted to wish me a "sweet" New Year!

The sentiment was much appreciated, but the cake called me all day! I didn't open it. Luckily, my friend Maryann came to visit me that night, and I sent it home with her. At least her kids and her parents would enjoy the cake. What's the point of all this? The point is: please, just send a card!

NAMETAGS! THEY'RE SIMPLE, CHEAP AND WORK!

WHAT IS SO difficult about keeping a collar with a nametag on a pet, especially a dog? This is a question that I have found myself asking repeatedly over the past few days. For some reason there has been a big increase in the number of lost dogs in the neighborhood, and none of them have collars or nametags! I don't understand this! If you love your pet, wouldn't you want to make sure that you got him back as quickly as possible if he were to wander off or get out of the house by accident? I have two nametags on my dogs, one on their collars and one on their harnesses. Perhaps this is a bit overboard but I'd rather be safe than sorry. Can there be any worse feeling in the world than to turn around and find out that your pet is gone without a nametag? I don't think so.

This is the story of Bobo, but it is also the story of so many other strays that I have found through the years and so many of the strays that are in the shelters. Countless times the endings are not happy, but this time, thankfully it was; but only because the dog ended up with me and I had the knowledge, patience and good sense not to let him out of my hands. Had he been brought to a shelter I don't think his owners would have been savvy enough to think to look there for the dog, and Bobo would have been ancient history—leaving the family to always wonder what happened, and Bobo to die a death he didn't deserve.

Bobo was brought to my office on a freezing cold February afternoon by two frantic Catholic school girls. They had him in a closed wooden box that was used to transport produce. They were frantically knocking at my office door yelling that they needed my help. As I got up from my desk to see what all the drama was about I noticed that they had a box. Whenever I see anyone with a box standing outside my office, they all seem to have that same look on their face: the look of "Please, I am desperate, take this animal off my hands!" When I opened the door, instantly I saw that look, but this time it was in stereo.

As I looked at the nervous faces of these two schoolgirls, I couldn't help but feel sorry for whatever it was that was in the box. The girls were so agitated and kept saying to me, "Be careful, it bites." What was "it"? They said a puppy. Seems that the puppy was almost committing doggie suicide by walking out into the very busy traffic of Third Avenue, and worse yet, at the very spot where the busy supermarket parking lot traffic exits into the street. Poor little dog would have been killed if it hadn't been for the kind and brave efforts of these two nice girls. As they grabbed the dog, he became spooked and tried to bite them. It was out of fear, not viciousness. Someone from the supermarket came out and helped them secure the little imp in the produce crate, which then left the little dude smelling like old onions with bad teeth. Of course, word on the street is to bring any stray to me so, lo and behold, that's what they did. I couldn't turn them away, so I thanked them and congratulated them on doing a great thing. They then told me that they had to run to dance class and that they were late, so off they went.

I opened the crate to find a very confused, old, frail, shivering little dog. As I looked him in the eyes I realized that he was not only old but blind! I felt terrible. How does an old, blind dog get lost? I looked to see if there were any tags under his scruffy little fur, and of course I came up empty. This is why I get really annoyed with people who don't keep collars with nametags on their dogs. Now I was stuck with this nervous little bundle of energy. Despite being a very old fellow, he paced back and forth in my office for hours. I was getting both dizzy and anxious watching him. I also realized as time went on that the little dude was deaf, too! Poor old guy! I was really concerned that he was dumped and that I was going to get *really* stuck with him. When I say stuck I don't mean it in a derogatory way, I just mean that I need a fourth dog like I need a hole in my head. I tried to give my new little pal some water, and he wouldn't touch it. I tried to give him some food in a bowl and the same thing, he wouldn't touch it.

As the hours passed, I sent out emails to all my friends to ask them to keep their eyes open for a sign about this shaggy little dog. He looked to be a Yorkie mix: gray, beige and dark brown. He was not neutered and was missing some teeth. I called the local police precinct, all the local vets and even the Animal Care and Control to make a report of a found pet and to see if he had been reported lost, which he hadn't! I lost an entire afternoon of work trying to re-unite my little friend with his owner. Then I called one of my volunteers, and good friend, Karen. I asked her to do me the favor of taking the sad little guy to the vet's office to see if he was micro-chipped. She showed up a little while later, picked up my little buddy and put him inside her coat to keep him warm. Then she drove him to the vet's office where we were disappointed to learn that he was not chipped! She weighed him while she was there, and he was a measly nine and a half pounds.

While Karen was away, a van from the ACC shelter pulled up in front of my office, and the driver knocked on my door. Someone from the supermarket had called in the dog and referred her to me. I opened the door to find Nora, a really kind "dog-catcher" that I had met at a few adoption events. She had no idea that she would be seeing me at the door when she knocked so she was quite surprised. We exchanged pleasantries and then I said, half kidding but seriously, "I know why you're here, and you can't have him." She started to laugh and asked me where he was. I told her that Karen had taken him to the vet to be scanned and that I would never surrender a frail little guy like him to the shelter. She was happy to hear that and knew that the little guy was in safe hands with me. Once again, we were proof that the "it takes a village" concept works when practiced. I quickly reassured Nora that I had the situation under control. She left and I closed the door, waiting for Karen to return with my little dude.

When she brought him back to me, I decided that if I couldn't find his owner or someone wonderful to take him that Sal and I would keep him until his time was up. After all, this dog looked so old and pathetic that he deserved to be treated well for his remaining time, although he was still quite peppy in terms of walking. Remember, he paced the full length of my office for hours and upon his arrival back from the vet, resumed the pacing where he had left off!

At 7:30 p.m. I decided to call it a day and headed home with my tiny, shivering bundle of a pooch. Sal had met me at the office and was walking along with us. He is so sappy and sensitive when it comes to these types of situations. As we got to our house, I saw my neighbor Carole and stopped to show her the little dude that I was affectionately calling Peppy. I told her to keep her eyes open for signs. In the meantime, Sal had walked ahead and had set up a playpen in our dining room for the little dude to hang out in while he was getting used to our house and all the four-legged friends that come with it. When I walked in I tried to put Peppy in the playpen while we had dinner. He was having none of it. He acted like someone was killing him. This lasted for all of three minutes.

Thank goodness that my own dogs are so used to "new friends" visiting. After the initial sniffing stuff is over, they could care less about him and all went about their evening ritual—sitting with Sal and I on the couch watching American Idol! Peppy paced the full length of our house for three solid hours. Sal and I were exhausted and sad watching him. We couldn't seem to get him to relax or settle down no matter what we tried. His little tail was tucked firmly under his belly the entire time, clearly reinforcing just how unhappy he was. The one thing that saved me from really losing my mind was that he wasn't hyperventilating, but rather he was breathing normally. When it came time for us to go to sleep, Sal picked the little dude up in his arms, and I decided it was important that I try him with food one last time. This time I put the wet food on my fingers and put it to his lips. Immediately he lapped it up. The poor little guy was ravenous. His owners must only hand feed him, and that was what he was used to! I was only too happy to spend the next few minutes filling his empty little belly with some much needed nutrition. He had to have paced five miles since I had taken him in that afternoon and there was no way he wasn't feeling starved and exhausted. After he finished devouring the food from my fingers he immediately seemed peaceful! Sal placed him on a big, cushy comforter on the floor, and he was only too happy to relax and call it a night! *Finally!* We both let out a huge sigh of relief. Each of us had been thinking it was going to be a really long night if we couldn't have gotten him to settle down, so this was a very welcomed sight!

Peppy slept like an angel through the entire night. At 6 a.m. he woke Sal up by standing on his back legs and leaning up on the bed, staring at him. Sal reached over, picked him up, placed him under the covers with him, and Peppy gladly fell back to sleep for another half hour until it was time to get up for the day. We decided that it was way too cold to take him for a walk with us and the "guys" so we left him home covered in blankets while we took our guys out. As we walked along in the freezing cold, Sal and I were saying how lucky it was for the little dog that he ended up with us for the night and not still outside someplace or in the shelter. No sooner did we get those words out that we saw a single, solitary sign on a pole—two blocks from our home—it was a picture of Peppy and some contact numbers for him. The sign said he was fourteen and blind. I would have guessed at least twelve, so I was close. This was the one morning that neither of us had cell phones with us so we had to memorize the number and call when we got home. As we hurried back to the house, we were almost giddy with excitement. Can there be anything better than reuniting a lost pet with the owner?

When we got in I immediately called the cell phone number that we had memorized from the sign. I got the voicemail, so I left a message. After all, it was not even 7:00 a.m. yet, so perhaps the person was sleeping or in the shower. No sooner did I hang up when the phone began to ring. It was the owner's boyfriend. He said that his girlfriend had been crying all night long and that they would be right over to get the dog, whose name it turned out was Bobo. Within ten minutes a thin Chinese girl was at the door with a young guy. I answered the door with the pooch in my arms. As soon as he got their scent he went crazy. The poor, homesick dog began to screech and wag his tail with such vigor that we couldn't even see it. He jumped from my arms and into his mommy's arms! Then he covered her face with kisses! The girl and I both began to get a little teary. I said to her that if she had only had a nametag on the poor dog she would have had him back in a matter of minutes, but instead both she and the dog had to suffer! She explained to me that her parents lived with her and didn't believe in leaving a collar on the dog in the house. I told her that she needed to have a long chat with them about the importance of having a nametag on the dog and how the poor fellow was so heartbroken without them and that this could have all been so easily avoided, had he had a tag!

I hope anyone reading this will think twice about not having a nametag on their beloved pet. The pain that both the owner and the pet experience during this kind of separation is beyond description and yet so simply avoidable! Think, just *think*.

DECEMBER 2005

Chestnut

WHEN I FIRST met Chestnut, it was a fluke. We didn't have an adoption event scheduled, but rather the ACC was doing an event in the next town over, Sunset Park. The person hosting the event for them did a miserable job promoting it and the turnout was evidence of that. About two hours into the event I received a desperate call from Latisha, the offsite event coordinator for the ACC. By now, we had become good friends. She was super stressed out. There she was at the event, with a bus filled with dogs and cats but with no volunteers to unload the dogs and show them, and, even worse than that, no one to show them to. The dogs were flipping out on the bus and the longer they were kept in the cages the more agitated they were becoming. Her heart was breaking. The last thing she wanted to do was to go back to the shelter with a full bus. She was pleading with me for help. She was especially concerned about Chestnut. I could hardly understand her as she tried to explain to me her dilemma and Chestnut's story. In the background the panicked barking of fifteen dogs in cages was making it almost impossible for me to hear her. From the few words I did catch, I understood that she had a badly abused dog and needed to get someone to adopt it as soon as possible.

When the call came in, I was enjoying a wonderful brunch with my husband in a new, pretty little coffee shop that was surrounded by windows. I was enjoying the bright December sun on my back and the first Sunday that I had off in a very long time. I had left the house in my most comfortable pair of sweats and had no makeup on. I was telling Sal how I didn't ever remember being so tired in my life. I was thinking how nice a warm shower and a copy of the *New York Times* to read while relaxing would feel when I got home. I had myself all psyched up to enjoy this much needed afternoon of downtime. But upon hearing the desperation in Latisha's voice, I felt infused with energy and my overwhelming desire to help save those animals kicked into high gear. We cut our brunch short, quickly paid the check and power-walked back to my office two blocks away and began to reach out to as many of our volunteers as we could. It was two weeks before Christmas, and everyone had things to do. Unbelievably, within one hour I was able to mobilize seven of my volunteers and secure a large parking spot for the bus to pull into on the avenue. I also made up tons of fliers and posted them on the nearby poles and distributed them to the local shops that so kindly help me promote my events; the liquor store, cupcake shop and deli. I then raced home and took the fastest shower of my life. Within one hour, the bus was parked on the avenue, the volunteers were unloading the dogs and we were well on our way to saving the day.

That's when I met Chestnut. Chestnut was the last dog to be loaded off the bus. He was terrified. There was no other way to describe it. God Bless Latisha. She is a wonderful lady with a heart bursting with love and compassion for these animals. Latisha kneeled on the floor of the bus and coaxed him out of the cage while gently pulling him toward her. Once out of the cage, he suctioned himself to the floor and just kept looking up at us with absolute terror in his eyes. This dog was the prettiest I had ever seen. He was a gorgeous, rich, light brown color and had the biggest, most shiny greenish eyes I had ever seen. To witness the fear in this dog was to witness the damage done by the awful acts of despicable human beings. This young pup had been so badly beaten and abused that he trusted no one. It took us quite a while to convince this beautiful fellow that we loved him and would never hurt him.

Once Chestnut was off the bus, he seemed to be a little more comfortable. My sister-in-law Judy took charge of this truly beautiful fellow. Her heart was broken thinking of how terrible this dog's life had been, and she was anxiously trying to get someone special to look kindly upon him to make up for all that had been done wrong. After a very short time, Mirella showed up with Sienna. Mirella had adopted Sienna, another beautiful pup from us a few months before. Sienna was doing so well. She was a very well adjusted, happy pup who loved to play with all dogs. Chestnut was very happy to meet her and was instantly at ease with her. Sienna seemed to understand that Chestnut was special, and she played so gently with him at first. They were very similar looking and kept kissing each other's face very softly. They were a match made in heaven. Eventually, as they got more comfortable with each other, Chestnut's tail began to wag and he started to jump around a little with excitement. We all let out a sigh of relief upon seeing that. There was hope for this little guy. His spirit hadn't been broken after all, and with some love and reassurance, he would be a wonderful, confident little pooch.

Mirella and Sienna stayed for quite a while. Mirella toyed with the idea of fostering Chestnut, but I was not certain it was wise to leave these two dogs alone in an apartment all day while she worked. They were beginning to play a little rough, and I was afraid that perhaps Chestnut might have a flashback to being abused and would hurt Sienna if the play fighting got too rough. Mirella agreed and decided that she would keep tabs on Chestnut and if he was still available at the end of the week she would go get him because she had a full week of vacation and would be home to supervise these two clowns at play. Monday came and went. My day just flew by and I never got a chance to post Chestnut in the window. On Tuesday I got a call from Latisha telling me how she *really needed* to get the dog a foster home or a forever home *ASAP.* I posted two pictures in my window, one of Chestnut looking head on into the camera showing how gorgeous he was and the other of him kissing his friend Sienna. I also included Chestnut's sad story.

Mirella stopped in and began to talk to me about the dog. She, like so many of my volunteers, couldn't get him out of her head. She was crazy for him, and it broke her heart to think of him in a cage instead of getting the love he so badly needed. She told me that she was probably going to go and get him on Saturday but it was only Tuesday and so much can happen in a shelter in four days—good and awful. At this point, the shelter was being plagued by pneumonia. An alarmingly high number of the dogs and cats were catching it. At the time, two dogs that I had adopted from previous events were extremely sick, in the animal hospital and receiving oxygen therapy. I was so worried that he would be the next victim of this illness. That evening, as I sat working in my office, I was lucky enough to have a man named Bill visit me. He had just read my window and was interested in Chestnut! I was so excited. I went over Chestnut's story with him, and as he listened to the details he was so kind and sympathetic. He didn't seem too thrilled about going to the shelter, but I gave him all the info on the dog anyway, said a prayer and kept my fingers crossed.

The next evening I was showing a home to a client in Bensonhurst. It was cold, dark and the second day of the NYC Transit Strike. Most people were in a stressed out mood because of the approaching holidays, the cold weather and the faltering economy. I was just hoping that I would be lucky enough to finally sell this home that had been a thorn in my side. As I showed the kitchen for the fiftieth time, my cell phone rang. I didn't recognize the number but answered it anyway. It was Bill. He was so excited. He had just adopted my boy Chestnut and wanted to share the wonderful news with me. Instantly I was laughing. This was great news and the Christmas present that I had been hoping for. He said that poor Chestnut was obviously terrified but that he was certain that in no time at all he would be able to transform him into a happy, loved, confident pup. My client must have thought that I was flaky because I was ecstatic and to non-animal people, what was the big deal, a dog got a home? To me, it was *almost* as good as being told that I could eat all the chocolate I wanted and never gain an ounce!

I finished showing the house and couldn't wait to return to my office. Once there, I began to make the calls. I love to share wonderful news with my volunteers, and Judy was the first one. She was thrilled. She then shared with me how she had cried on Sunday night thinking about our beautiful boy and that sometimes these events were just so hard for her. I have to agree that it is tough, but when we are able to have a success story like this, the pain is worth it.

The next day Bill dropped into my office to give me an update. I could see from the smile on his face and the look in his eyes that rescuing this dog was as good for him as it was for Chestnut. He was so happy and said what a great dog he was, that already he was beginning to wag his tail and show signs of being comfortable with his new life.

About a month had passed since Bill had adopted Chestnut when I received a call from one of my volunteers who had been at that very sad event. She was jubilant. The reason for her call was to tell me that she had met Bill and Chestnut on the shore and that she recognized Chestnut from his incredible eyes, but as for his confidence—she would never know he was the same dog. In just that short period of time Bill had worked wonders. Chestnut was a playful, confident fellow who looked and acted as though he never had a bad day in his life.

The very next day, Bill came into my office with a very distressed look on his face. Alarmed, I said, "How's Chestnut?" He slowly and sadly shook his head from side to side. My heart began to sink! Then he said that Chestnut was wonderful *but* his building's management company had sent him a letter saying that if the dog didn't go, they both would have to go! Bill's lease says "no pets," *however,* half of the tenants in the building have dogs and all of their leases say "no pets." Bill was crushed and had contacted an attorney. He said that he had no intentions of giving Chestnut away and that the dog deserved to be able to stay. He did nothing wrong, didn't bark, wasn't destructive and was very well-mannered to everyone in the halls and on the elevators. The attorney said it would cost about $3000 to represent Bill in court. Bill, for a while, tried to ignore the letter because upon speaking with other tenants in the building with pets, he learned that everyone else ignored the letter and the "issue" seemed to go away!

Unfortunately, Bill was sent another, more threatening letter telling him that he had to get rid of the dog. After much discussion with his attorney, he felt that he didn't really have much choice. The way the law worked, if Bill had had the dog for ninety days and no one said anything to him, he would have been able to keep him. But, because he got his letter early into his ownership of the dog, his chances of winning were almost slim to none. Bill was crushed. The only bright spot to this story is that Bill had a woman friend whose seventeen year old dog had just passed away, and she was only too happy to give Chestnut the forever home he deserved. At least for Chestnut and this lady the ending is a happy one. As for Bill, he did a wonderful thing by taking Chestnut from the shelter. He showed him that not all people are mean and cruel and that it was possible for Chestnut to be unconditionally loved and to unconditionally love; for that he should feel great.

DECEMBER 11, 2005

Skip Shopping, Come Adopting Adoption Event

THE MORNING OF this event was probably one of the calmer mornings we had before any other event. We had relatively little to set up, and we were starting later than usual. As I got into my car, a man passing by pointed out to me that my passenger side mirror on my car was hanging off. Someone had intentionally broken it. I wasn't happy, but I didn't bother to dwell on it or let it mess up my mood. I had a big day ahead of me and hoped that by the time I was driving home I would be filled with the same feeling of accomplishment and success that I am usually filled with at the end of one of our events.

We were hosting the "Skip Shopping, Come Adopting Adoption Event" two weeks after "The Paws to Give Thanks" event. It was all outdoors, which made for a very cold, long day. We were to be part of a Support the Troops Holiday Celebration that was taking place in a park located under the Verrazano Bridge and at the front entrance of the Ft. Hamilton Army Base. The people hosting the event really needed help decorating the park. So along with two of my volunteers, Karen and Judy, I had spent the Friday night before decorating in the freezing temps. We placed bows all around the fences, assembled mechanical deer decorations and hung garland. It was very cold that night, but we were getting pumped at the idea of having a wonderful turnout at this event over the next two days and hoped that Sunday, for our event, it would be packed with potential adopters. I was relying on the publicity efforts of the people hosting the Holiday Celebration to draw the crowd. I had put out very few fliers compared to our usual thousands. It wasn't until the evening before the event, when I was at the Saturday portion of the two day affair, that I realized that they didn't have the kind of turnout that I *needed* or expected at my event.

I left the event, raced back to my office, made two hundred more fliers and off we went! My husband and I scrambled to post as many fliers on poles as we could so that the next day perhaps some people would show up. It was freezing cold and the wind was brisk, making it very painful on the fingers to put up fliers. Scotch tape and mittens don't jive, so the fingers must be naked.

The next day was very brisk. My volunteers and I showed up at the park a half hour before the bus pulled up. We were all ready for the long day, dressed in plenty of layers! The normally large crowds that we attract were not there, and this was causing us to be a little worried about our numbers! We had gotten so spoiled with the lines of potential adopters we typically draw! When the bus pulled in we had only a handful of people interested in adopting. There was the usual North Shore Animal League bus and a van from the ACC, both filled to capacity. We had a big job ahead of us. When the van was opened, the first little creatures to be off-loaded were a stunning litter of six, two month old pure-Pit puppies. Most of them were chocolate colored with a thin little line of white going down the center of their face. The others were a soft fawn color with a little black outlining the ears and face. They were super sweet and so cuddly. The oohing and ahhing that was going on as we were unloading them was great. As Latisha, the Off-Site Event Coordinator for the ACC and now one of my good buddies, unloaded them one at a time, she handed them off to me. I put a red or green bandana around each little neck and then we wrapped them in soft, cuddly blankets that we happened to have on hand. Six lucky volunteers got to spend some time holding on to these adorable little guys and gals. Within the first two hours, five of the six were adopted out. Then, after a little while, one of the people who adopted two of the others came back and adopted the last pup for her friend! Six great adoptions right there!

When we began to unload the dozen plus dogs from the bus, it turned out that we had two dogs back from our last event. They were both named Baby. "Brown Baby" was a beautiful two year old Chocolate Lab/Greyhound Mix. She was a tall, lean dog who pranced beautifully as she walked. With a soulful face and fabulous disposition, I felt that she was a dog that should have easily found a home. She was neat looking in all ways. The other Baby was "Momma Baby." She was the brindle Pit who had recently given birth. Her boobs were still hanging, and her mood was just as droopy. She was less than happy to be out in the freezing cold and just wanted to sit on her handler's lap all day, swaddled in a coat, and that's what she did. Why not, it could be her last day on this earth, why not let her have her own way?

It's funny how things work out sometimes. In late November a woman had passed by my office and dropped off a large bag of things that had belonged to her dog that had just passed. Initially I looked at the bag and thought, "Geez, where am I going to store this stuff?" But as the event approached and the weather grew colder, I realized that in the bag were many doggie coats. I decided to bring them to the event with me because I knew we would get good use out of them. Also my volunteer Karen had a bunch of doggie coats in her car, so between the two of us we had a good amount of coats to keep the dogs somewhat warm during the long five hour day. It wasn't until I looked around and saw how wonderful it was to be able to make these poor shelter pets comfortable with those coats that I realized what a great thing this owner did. Her dog's memory lived on in the coats that she gave to me and allowed me to help these less fortunate guys and gals! If we hadn't had the coats these poor animals would have been very uncomfortable.

At one point in the day I saw the woman who had donated the coats to me and made a point of going over to her to thank her and let her know how super it was for us to have had those coats on hand! This brings me back to the village thing again. It is something that one will see over and over in my book: how important it is to have people contributing and working together for the good of the pets! Together we can and do make a difference!

We had a bunch of sick animals at our event that day but only one was *obviously* sick. Blackie, a young pup, was pooping pure blood continuously. The poor dog's belly was constantly contracting, and she was arching her back making almost a "C" shape with her body. We ached for her! She was so uncomfortable and so sick and yet stuck at this event for five hours. We put a nice warm jacket on her and tried to make her feel better by giving her some much needed attention. We were really concerned about her, and it broke my heart that we couldn't adopt her out that day. Because she was obviously sick, she had to be brought back to the shelter and checked out by the medical department. Who knew what would happen then?

Then there was Lacy. Lacy was a very non-descript brown dog. She was only eight months old and on the small side. She kept her tail down all day and looked just plain miserable. I didn't know if she was overwhelmed by all the noise and the cold or if she was sick. We had a sweater on her, but I don't think it was enough to keep the really frigid temps from invading her body. Towards the very end of the day two young Hispanic girls came along and adopted her. We were so happy. This poor little thing needed to go home to a nice warm house that night, not back on an ice cold bus and back to an ice cold shelter.

About a week passed and I got a call. It was from the people who had adopted Lacy. It turned out that Lacy was extremely sick and knocking on death's door. The new owners were frantic, trying to save her life. It was a long, tough road for Lacy, and had she not been adopted by these kind people she probably would have died within the week, if she wasn't euthanized before then.

Sometimes we get dogs with issues, and such was the case of Rosie, a very loveable, four-year old Beagle who was owner surrendered. Owner surrendered dogs seem to be the most disappointed and depressed of all the dogs. They have such a look of heartbreak over having been betrayed by the people that they would have died protecting. It is a look that has become all too familiar to me at these events. I usually try to guess at the dog's history before reading their information page just by looking at their eyes. I am usually on the money with my guess. Rosie's issue was that she *hated* kids—not just disliked, but hated. We had to make sure that no one with kids came near her. She made no bones about it, when a child approached she went nuts. In order to keep kids from trying to pet Rosie we tried to keep her moving. As I was taking her for a spin around the park I was stopped by a lovely woman named Ida who worked for the Parks Department. Ida began to cry when she saw Rosie and how sad she looked. She then reached into her pocket, pulled out her wallet and showed me a picture of her Noel. Noel and Rosie were dead ringers for each other! Noel had just died, and Ida was missing her something awful. Ida hadn't expected to be passing by the event and had no money to pay the adoption fee for Rosie but didn't want to miss the chance to give her a good home. I asked Ida if she had children, and she said no, she lived alone with her other pets. Sounded good to me! I paid the adoption fee and told her she could pay me back at a later date. Ida was thrilled, and Rosie seemed to realize that she was getting a good home, so her tail went up high and began to wag.

We also had a terrier mix named Lima. Lima was a very pretty dog that kind of reminded me of an Airedale mixed with a Shepherd. She had a cute little bearded face and weighed about forty-five pounds. She was a nice-sized dog, not small but not big. Lima was so unusual looking that I got a kick out of her. She was very well-behaved, kind of on the mellow side and seemed to like all other dogs. Lima enjoyed sitting on the park bench with her handler. As the day was winding down, the temps were falling even more and fewer and fewer people were coming by. We were becoming discouraged by the prospect of having to send Lima back. Finally a woman that I recognized from the area came by with her eighty-ish mom. They had an elderly poodle at home and were looking to get another dog that wasn't too high energy. Lima was the perfect compliment. She was calm, quiet and sweet. We hadn't observed any behavioral issues all day, and she had been approached by many people. After spending some time with Lima, the woman and her mom decided to adopt her. Wow, such a feeling of relief! They filled out all the paperwork and walked her over to the car for the quick ride home. Lima was reluctant to leave her handler. She had bonded with the volunteer who had been kind to her all day and was sad to say goodbye. She was so stubborn that we had to have the volunteer go over to the car to reassure Lima that it was a good thing for her to get in the car with her new owners and that life would be good for her from here on. Finally Lima seemed to understand what was being said to her and hopped into the back seat. We all stood there waving to her as the car pulled away from the curb. The later in the day the adoption takes place the more emotional it is for us because we are painfully aware of just how close we came to sending the animal back! This was a close one!

When it was time to re-load the bus, we were putting back far too many for my liking. Baby, the momma, was loaded onto the bus with a great deal of sadness on the part of my volunteer, Anna. She and Rob, the dog trainer, had alternated holding her all day. She was a very sweet girl that just didn't exude fun when people looked at her. Anna and Rob had liked her from the previous event and then today, after spending all day with her, they were crazy about her. Anna decided that she would foster Baby and that she would go to the shelter the next day to complete the foster application and bring her home. But the one that will haunt me until the day I die is "Baby, Brown Baby." She was the chocolate Lab/Greyhound mix that had been at our previous event as well. Baby was so well behaved all day, but when it came time to load her onto the bus she went ballistic. She fought tooth and nail. It was as though she knew all of her chances were up and she was going back to die. The wailing that came from her cage is haunting. She is another chapter in this book. One that will cause you such pain as you read the story. I cried for days over this dog and like I said will remember her till the day I die. I hope that her story will encourage people to think about many things and thereby possibly save many more lives!

Overall the day was very successful, but as is always the case, there is a sadness that takes over the moment. The idea of sending back pets is gut-wrenching to all who are there to participate in that awful task of loading the dogs back on the bus. No matter how many we adopt out, sending even one back is painful. Add to that the scene that "Brown Baby" created and there will be tears, plenty of tears.

BABY

*T*his is the article I wrote about Baby for Home Reporter and Sunset Newspaper. *It was published on December 22, 2005. If it sounds angry it is because I was and am! Read on and see why.*

Deep sadness. What else can one say when just hours before she was going to be adopted, Baby died of what is believed to have been a heart attack brought on by the anxiety of being in a cage.

Baby was a wonderful two year old female Lab/Greyhound mix. We first met her at our Nov. 26th event. She was tall, elegant and simply regal. She boasted class and dignity. She was extremely well-behaved and tried so hard to win people over with her excellent behavior and ability to follow commands. This was a perfect dog. No one would consider her because she was "too big." But she really wasn't. She was just the size of a Lab and, personally, I don't think that is too big. It broke our hearts to send her back at the end of the day. We hoped that since she hadn't been in the shelter that long and that she exuded such poise and beauty, that she still had an excellent chance at finding a home.

When the bus pulled up to our Dec. 11th event, I was filled with very mixed emotions at seeing Baby once again. Part of me felt like, GEEZ, this poor thing has been sitting in that shelter for the past two weeks waiting for someone to finally see her beauty and give her a home, but then the other part of me said, at least she is still around to wag her tail and has the opportunity to once again show what a terrific, model-like dog she is.

The day was gray, cold and the turnout was not as we had hoped. Despite the bitter conditions, my dedicated volunteers worked tirelessly to promote all of these wonderful pets for five long hours. We supplied as many of the dogs with coats as we possibly could. By the end of the day, we had adopted out twenty of the twenty-nine pets. Much to my extreme disappointment, Baby was one of the ones we were going to have to put back on the bus. When that moment came, she resisted fiercely. Once we got her back in the bus, she let out a low whimper which then grew into a full-blown wail; one that all who heard will never forget. She was pleading with us to save her. It was as though she understood that she had just lost her last chance and wanted us to know that she didn't want to *die*. As we all stood around with tears rolling down our faces, there was nothing anyone could do. All of our volunteers are maxed out with pets. Heck, I am up to three dogs and four cats. So, with Baby begging to be saved, the bus closed its doors and started the sad journey to the shelter.

What I would like to come from this incredibly sad ending is to raise awareness. Please people, *think!* When you are surrendering an animal to a *kill* shelter, or any other shelter for that matter, consider something other than yourself. Consider how your pet is going to feel when you drive away. Consider what your pet's day is going to be like until they are either killed or adopted and how long will it take. Are they going to be happy, anxious, heartbroken, mistreated? Most importantly, ask yourself if you did everything you possibly could to re-home your pet before you took that trip to the shelter? Surrendering a pet to a shelter is not something that should be taken lightly! You need to realize that the ultimate fate of that animal is still your responsibility and that just because you dropped it off at the shelter and drove away, the story doesn't end there. For your pet, it is the beginning of what is a whole other chapter whose ending may not be a good or happy one. Can you live with that? Don't you owe your loyal furry friend more?

SOME BACKGROUND ON MY EFFORTS TO SAVE BABY

I WORKED SO HARD to try to find Baby a home. She was that beautiful. After experiencing her begging us to save her life as we put he on the bus that Sunday night, I was tormented by the sounds that she produced from deep within her soul. All throughout the night, I kept hearing the desperation in her voice. I couldn't shake it. So, on Monday morning, I called Latisha at the shelter. She told me that the dog's time was up and that I needed to do something ASAP. I begged her to give me more time and was able to get her to give Baby a five day reprieve. I made many phone calls on Monday and Tuesday, desperately trying to save Baby's life. I was able to get the local newspaper to agree to run her on the cover of Thursday's issue. Wednesday evening, I had someone going to look at her. It was the mother of someone who had adopted a kitty from me. She was confident that her mom would take the dog! She had shown her the picture and shared Baby's sad story, and the mom was really feeling for Baby.

Two hours before she was to be picked up at the shelter, Baby died. When Latisha called to tell me, all I could do was cry. I could hardly talk. I felt like I had been kicked in the stomach. All of the air just drained from my body. I felt sick. I was so close! I immediately thought that a mistake had been made and that my beautiful friend had been put to sleep. Latisha reassured me that that was not the case.

The next day was even worse. The local paper, true to their word, published Baby on the front page. She looked beautiful, and they told her sad story. The phone calls began to come into my office. So many kind hearted people wanted to help her out. They weren't really looking for a dog, but if it meant saving her life, they would be happy to help her out! I was so touched by the out-pouring of love, but with each phone call was forced to tell her sad story. I spent the whole day crying! I take the plight of these animals to heart, and, when I envision what I believe happened to this dog and how she made herself so anxious about being caged, I almost make myself sick. I am very claustrophobic and feel a strong empathy towards animals who share this fear.

What really made me feel bad about Baby's death, aside from the obvious, was that her owners surrendered her knowing that she had an anxiety problem. Did they give that any consideration? Did they even consider how that might impact her stay? I feel that I cried so many tears for their dog that they should be made aware of the terrible time she had, the anxiety she experienced and the ultimate role that it may have played in her death. I would like a minute to ask them a few questions, like did you do anything to try to re-home her yourself? Did you do all you could have to make her staying in your home possible? Did you ever think about her after surrendering her?

I hope that Baby's story will open the eyes of people considering surrendering their pet to a shelter. Shelters should not be for any Tom, Dick or Harry who decides that they don't want their pet anymore. But rather Tom, Dick and Harry should have to find their animals a home on their own. Shelters should exist for the down and out stray dogs and cats that are found on the street—the defenseless kittens that are born on the street and in backyards. They should not be for the selfish, irresponsible pet-owners who made the mistake of taking in a pet and realizing too late that it wasn't for them. If I sound angry it is because I am. Surrendering a pet to the shelter is not like returning a sweater to Bloomingdales, yet some people give it the same consideration. This mentality needs to change.

This is a copy of an article that I wrote for Spectator *on January 11, 2006 describing the plight of a senior dog that the owner could no longer care for. It worked—the dog got adopted.*

January 2006

Senior Dog Desperate For Home

When you do as many adoptions as my wonderful group of volunteers and I, each day is filled with many different kinds of pet related phone calls. Probably one in every twenty is a story of such sadness that it just takes over your day. Today was one of those days.

It all started with a call from the kind folks at the local church. Since we have held many of our events at the church, some people think that the church is actively involved in the placement of unwanted pets. While they are more than willing to accommodate our events, they don't get directly involved with placement. So, when someone left a message on their machine about a dog desperately needing a home, they forwarded the message to me and I immediately returned the call.

That is the phone call that broke my heart today. The voice on the other end was struggling for each and every breath. The caller was a lovely woman named Rose. At just fifty-one years old, Rose is suffering from severe asthma and possibly emphysema. She has tremendous difficulty talking without becoming completely winded. Walking without collapsing has become almost impossible for her. In addition to not being able to breathe she is plagued with severe anxiety attacks. Combine all of these conditions and it becomes impossible for her to care for her dog, Foxy. This is where the story gets even sadder.

Foxy is a seemingly healthy thirteen year old sweetie who looks like a fox. She is black and brown, weighs a mere forty pounds and is super friendly. Rose's breathing is so labored that she can no longer walk Foxy. Because of this, she is being faced with the awful, heart-wrenching prospect of surrendering Foxy to the only Animal Shelter in Brooklyn that will take her—Animal Care and Control (ACC).

The ACC is a kill shelter that is almost always overcrowded with unwanted pets. Because the shelter is contracted by the city to take in every dog or cat that is being surrendered they cannot turn anyone away. The only way to make room for new ones is to euthanize pets that have not been adopted. Think about it . . . the chances of someone coming into a kill shelter and adopting a thirteen year old dog are as likely as snow in NYC in June. So essentially, if surrendered, thirteen year old Foxy will spend the last few days of her life in a cold cage surrounded by frantic, anxious dogs barking incessantly and being passed over continually by prospective adopters. After being traumatized and repeatedly disappointed for a week or whatever amount of time it takes, then the time will come for her cage to be given to a newcomer and she will be euthanized for no other reasons than lack of space and her owner's extremely unfortunate and sad inability to care for her. A cruel reality for Foxy!

Rose is heartbroken over this and is begging for help in finding a good home. I will have a picture of Foxy in the next day or so, and would be very happy if anyone out there would consider helping Rose breathe easier knowing that Foxy has a place to relax and be loved in her golden years. At thirteen years old Foxy deserves a non-traumatic end. She deserves to wind down her time on a comfy sofa taking afternoon naps with her owner. Don't you agree? Is there anyone who would enjoy the company of a sweet, calm and gentle senior pooch? If so, please call me. *Thanks* so much.

So the article was printed, and I nervously awaited a response. Oh, the power of newspaper coverage. This story ran two weeks in a row—the second time with a picture. Pictures truly are worth a thousand words and can convey a message like nothing else. I got a call from a woman who works for a local real estate management company. We have spoken of pets before; she had helped me place one in the past. Her name was Maggie, and she had a heart of gold. Maggie was so touched by Foxy's sad story that she offered to foster her for me until I found a forever home. I was thrilled but apprehensive at the same time. Suppose I couldn't find a taker, then what?

Reluctantly I agreed to take her up on her offer. I put her in touch with Rose, and they made plans for Maggie to pick up Foxy on a Saturday afternoon. Foxy hit it off famously with Maggie's dog, Houdini, and all was going really well. Maggie took Foxy to the vet because she had a bladder infection and needed some meds. The vet thought that Foxy was even older than the thirteen years Rose had said, and that would make her even more difficult to place.

Maggie called me a few days into it and told me that things could not be going better. She thought that Foxy was a terrific dog who was really adjusting to her new situation beautifully. Of course this phone call made me so happy. I had been concerned that an old dog like that might have real issues adjusting to another dog and a new home and owner. But Foxy was rolling with it. I promised Maggie that I would continue to make calls and ask people to adopt Foxy and that I would try to re-home her as quickly as I could. Maggie told me not to rush, that the dog was no bother and that she was enjoying her.

Two days later I got the call that dreams are made of. It was Maggie saying that she was crazy for Foxy and that there was no way that she could give Foxy away to anyone. She said that Foxy was a wonderful dog who had gotten so comfortable with her new situation that it would be a crime to uproot her. She said that Foxy deserved to stay with her and Houdini until her time was up. Could I ever have hoped for a better ending? No way. Now I could call Rose with the wonderful news that Foxy had a forever home with a fantastic new owner and even better than that, she had a companion to keep her company all day while Maggie worked. Houdini was a welcoming, easy going soul, making Foxy's stay a true pleasure. This is what makes all this animal conversion stuff so rewarding—moments like this, when good people step up to the plate to help out and then go above and beyond, as Maggie did!

The winter passed and Foxy and Houdini were really enjoying each other's company. Maggie took Foxy with her on the weekends to visit her relatives, and Foxy was loved by one and all. She had a disposition that was one in a million, and Maggie felt that she was the lucky one to have been able to take in Foxy and not the other way around. Each phone call I got from Maggie to give me an update about the dog was even better than the previous. Things were perfect. Perfect until April, when Foxy developed cancer. She dropped weight rapidly and became very frail. Maggie was crushed. She had nicknamed Foxy Grandma, and it was killing her that Grandma was failing so quickly. Within a month, poor Foxy had to be put to sleep. Maggie called me that following morning to give me the details. Together we cried on the phone as she relayed to me Foxy's last moments and how she took her to the park before bringing her to be put down. She wanted Foxy to go one last time to her favorite place. Maggie also brought Rose, Foxy's previous owner, with her to the vet for those last moments. It was a very sad time for Rose and for Maggie, but Maggie truly felt blessed for having had the opportunity to spend those few short months with a dog that was one in a million. As for Houdini, sadly he walked around the apartment for days after Foxy's passing with a, "Where's my Grandma?" look on his face.

SOFIA

The cat with the bad girl attitude

SAL AND I can't remember exactly what year we took Sofia in, but we think it was back in 1999. Sofia was brought to my attention by my neighbor, Carole. It was a cool October night, and Carole saw Sofia hanging around when she was out walking her dog Toto. She felt sorry for her and decided to call me so I could see her. Now back in 1999, I hadn't established myself as the neighborhood sucker for every stray animal yet. Nope, I was still working undercover. When Carole called and said that there was something she wanted me to see, and to come outside, I should have known that it had four legs and fur and needed a home. But that's okay, since then I have suckered Carole into *three* new pets so, seeing the handful that Sofia turned out to be, we are even.

Sofia was hanging around outside pretending to be a sweet kitty. She was about eight or nine months old and very pretty. She had very deep brown stripes and big eyes. She made herself out to be a very nice cat, but that could not have been farther from the truth. She was the devil in disguise. I went out to say hello, and she was all full of love for me, purring like crazy and circling around my legs. She allowed me to pick her up, and she seemed to be a very nice little kitty that had somehow gotten away from her owner. Having three cats already, I didn't feel like I needed a fourth, so I didn't offer to take her in. I was concerned about any new additions because we had an old, sickly cat named Kookie, and we were concerned about upsetting her.

Sofia seemed quite content to sit on my porch and hang out among the flowers in our garden. I hoped that she knew her way back home and after petting her for a little while went back inside to watch the 11:00 p.m. news. Since it was a nice October night, we had our windows open, and Sofia could hear the TV and us talking. After about a half hour she decided that she wanted to come inside. She sat outside our window and complained as loudly as she could. I went back outside, fed her and then tried to explain to her that she needed to go back home to her mommy and that her mommy must be missing her. Then I went back inside. Sal, being smarter than me when it comes to these things, didn't venture outside. He knows that once you make contact with one of these strays it's all over. They become our "problem." As far as he was concerned, we didn't need any "problems" at that moment. He was right.

After the news ended, we turned off the TV, closed the window and headed downstairs to the bedroom. We didn't know that Sofia remained outside of our living room window crying all night long! Unfortunately for the neighbors across the street, they have their bedrooms in the front of the house and were stuck listening to her relentless heartbreaking, lonely cries. Needless to say, they all thought she belonged to us because she was sitting on our porch. We got an earful the next day. We tried to tell everyone that she wasn't ours, but they didn't care. They said that we needed to take her in or find her a home. So, we took her in.

For the first few months, we kept her upstairs in an extra bedroom. We took care of having her tested, fixed and hoped to find her a home. But, unfortunately, there were no takers. We were afraid to mix her with the other cats because she was much younger and, by this point, had shown her fresh side to us. About three months later, Kookie ended up dying. She had gotten cancer and deteriorated quickly. She was fifteen years old, and we were heartbroken. But, once Kookie was gone, we decided that we could mix Sofia with the other cats and see how it went. It didn't go well. Sofia was a real witch. She walked around hissing, spitting and growling like a dog. She was awful to the other cats and to Gallagher. We didn't know what to do with her. We hoped that she would mellow with time and that perhaps her "bad girl attitude" was just a facade that she was putting up out of fear.

One day Sofia was able to run past me and out into the yard. I was so afraid that she would get lost, but was unable to get her to come back inside. She disappeared into a neighbor's yard and that was the end of her for the next few hours. Sal and I went out to eat and when we came home, there she was sitting on the welcome mat in the front of the house patiently waiting for us to let her back in. Soon this became her routine. She would sneak past us to get into the yard, disappear for an hour and then return to the front of the house. Our houses are attached, so she had to go down four houses and then down a common driveway to get to the front of our house. But she was so smart that she figured it all out in no time. I was amazed. How did she know which house was ours? All of the neighbors got to know her and got a kick out of watching her walk up and down the sidewalk! In Greek the word for Mrs. is Kyria, so we started to call her Kyria Sofia because she was like a smart little old woman, the way she roamed the block!

Kyria Sofia turned out to be a super smart cat. If she wanted to come back inside and no one came to the front of the house to open the door for her she would then come back to the yard and wait until she saw me come into the back room. Then she would jump up onto the window sill and pull the screen towards her with her claws. She did this until I noticed she was there. She also proved to be fearless. Her "bad girl attitude" was genuine. She feared no one and nothing. When Carole would walk by with Toto, Kyria Sofia would wait in the bushes and then jump out as they passed and "Benny Hill" Toto (quick slaps on his head).

Kyria also showed herself to be quite the welcoming committee. One summer my mother-in-law had new tenants moving in. Sofia watched the moving men going in and out and then decided that she wanted to be part of the scene. So she snuck upstairs into the apartment and showed herself around. She made herself at home among all the boxes. After the moving men left, the young couple who had just moved in decided to take a break and sat down in the living room to have a soda. As they are just starting to relax, out of the corner of their eye they see a cat. They look at each other and start laughing. They had no idea that the apartment came with a cat! After a short while Sofia started showing her true colors, and they were only too happy to open the door and let her go. Not long after that day I was standing outside chatting with the new neighbors, when along came Sofia walking up the steps. The girl started laughing and asked me if I knew who owned that cat. I smiled, rolled my eyes and said, "What did she do this time?" She then proceeded to tell me the story of how Sofia had snuck into their apartment.

I hate allowing Sofia out of the house, but we have to. If we don't let her out for her daily hour-long jaunt, she becomes like a rebellious, PMS-ing teenager. She whines, complains and screams the word "no" perfectly. She climbs up our French door and hits the fancy handle with her paws trying to open it. She is so persistent that we have no choice but to give in. We have tried the whole water gun thing, but it turns out the little Kyria loves water!

Sofia has also figured out how to open the basement windows. We used to love to have them open but with the screens in place. Unfortunately, the little witch was able to figure out how to slide the windows from side to side to open them. No longer can we leave those basement windows open because we have to worry about her liberating the other cats!

Over the past few years Sofia has mellowed a little bit. While she still "talks" to herself as she walks through the house, she doesn't do as much spitting and hissing as she used to. I am sure the other cats are grateful for that.

MACHI CAMACHI

ACHI CAMACHI JOINED our petting zoo as kitty number four. Having never been a cat person, I cannot believe that I have four. Four cats and three dogs, we can kiss any vacation plans goodbye for the next twenty years! Who in their right mind would assume responsibility for this kind of insanity? There are some days, when the cats are busting the dogs' chops or vice versa and things are a little nutty, that I look around and think, what have I done to myself?

Machi Camachi, like most of our crew, was a very unintentional new addition. His original owners had him for over a year and loved him. He was a huge, de-clawed, dark tiger-striped kitty, and a very handsome one at that. His owners, like so many other owners, had to give him up because their infant child turned out to be deathly allergic to the poor fellow. Machi was surrendered to a vet's office, and somehow he ended up staying in a cage for six months! Imagine how a small cougar of a kitty felt going from king of his castle to a forgotten cat in a small, dingy cage in the basement of a vet's office. He was sad, very sad. As the six month mark was approaching, the vet wanted Machi out. Sadly, he had been there so long that no one knew his real name anymore.

It came to the point that the vet was threatening to turn Machi over to the ACC. Along comes Emily, a neighbor of mine, and a fellow animal lover. She happens to walk into my office and requests a de-clawed cat. I call this cat rescuer that I know and tell her that I had a request for a de-clawed cat and did she have any because I didn't. This is how I first heard about Machi. Diane, the cat rescuer hooks up Emily with Machi. Emily's three year old granddaughter names him

Tigerlily, which is really funny when we think about it. Machi is truly a handsome, not pretty, but handsome cat—and there she is calling him Tigerlily.

After the first day, Emily calls to say that the cat is not eating and she is worried. After a few days, she finally gets him to eat, and he is starting to get comfortable with them. Emily is thrilled. The grand-daughter is thrilled. The grandson, who lives with Emily, is thrilled. Everyone is happy with Tigerlily, and Tigerlily is happy with them. A match made in heaven. Then along comes day four. Day four was not magical; it turned out that everyone was allergic to Tigerlily. The asthma that had been dormant in the grandson came back! His doctor said the cat had to go. But go where? Emily was heartbroken, the kids were heartbroken, and I was stressed. The vet wouldn't take him back—Diane the rescuer who had made the match was too overwhelmed with other animals to take this one in, so this big, strapping fellow was dropped in my lap.

My husband has been the most patient person alive when it comes to me and my animal antics and is the one who got me into cats—so part of this is his fault. I call him and tell him the dilemma I am faced with and as usual, his response is, "Okay, so we'll take him." What a good guy! Talking to him about pets is like having a conversation with myself. There is always room at "The Inn," regardless of what we have to do to make it happen.

My husband had been studying for a very difficult test he had to take at the end of that week. It was already Tuesday, and he was stressing about it. He was in the midst of making a career change, becoming a teacher for the NYC Board of Education. Having been laid off from his Wall Street job in December because of outsourcing, he had not worked steadily in over eight months and was very anxious. To elevate his anxiety level even higher, he had met a friend who had taken this very same test, and she told him she failed it three times before finally passing it!

Sal took a break from studying, met me on the corner—cat carrier in hand, and we went to get Tigerlily. Tigerlily was striking, like a real boy cat. We spent a few minutes trying to get acquainted with him and then attempted to get him into the carrier. We had a heck of a time. I realize now it was probably a tight fit for this hulking kitty, but at the time we were just focused on getting him into the carrier. Thankfully, the walk to our house was quick but he fought the whole time! I felt terrible. My original plan was to bring him to my office, let him hang around with me all day, and then I would bring him home. Once I realized what a traumatic event it was for both him and us to get him in the carrier, I knew that those plans would have to change. So Sal and I brought him to our home. We had a large size dog crate already set up in our dining room from a previous foster, so we put him in there with a litter box with Feline Pine Litter in it.

To say Tigelily was unhappy would be an understatement. He screamed bloody murder, which in turn agitated our "guys." After the first hour of screaming, poor Sal calls me at his wit's end. How could someone study with all this noise and animal anxiety going on around them? I knew how stressed he had been about studying for this test and now precious time was being wasted. This was backfiring on me. I was trying to do something good and now it was coming back to bite me. I tried to calm Sal down and surprisingly, it was very easy. He said he would try to talk to the cat. I was happy to hear that he was going to attempt a friendship with this distressed kitty rather than tell me to find it another home.

When I came home that night Machi was still losing his mind so we let him out of the cage figuring that if he were allowed to walk around he would be calmer. Initially, he was like a rabid animal. I was afraid of him. He made obscene noises and sounded like he was possessed. He also had some right hook! Now I understood why he was de-clawed. He could be lethal. A right hook like that with nails—forget about it! This guy was a powerhouse, and he was fast, too. I tried to make friends with him while he was under the dining room table. He gave me a quick right, left, right and left. My dogs are basically immune to new cats coming in to the house, so they barely gave him the time of day, but poor Machi was still terrified of them. He walked around low to the ground not knowing what to expect from them. He broke my heart.

It turns out that Machi didn't like Feline Pine Litter. His way of expressing his disapproval was not to use it. I can deal with fur on the floor, an occasional throw up and some tracked litter around the house, but poop and cat pee on my gorgeous, original parquet floors—no way! I was mad. This kitty wouldn't work out if that was what he did. I have been in houses that smell like cat pee. It is gross. I would never have a house like that, but, at the same time, I knew I had no one to take him, and he would be killed if I brought him to the shelter.

A few days passed and I found an old shoe box to give Machi to hang out in. I took the box, sprinkled some cat nip in it and put in on the floor where he was sitting. I walked away and figured that I would let him decide if this was something he would enjoy. After a few minutes, I heard him scratching in the box. I walked in just in time to see him peeing in the box. I wait for him to take a marathon pee in the box and grab it. Of course the box has a leak and the urine is spilling all over the room as I try to get to the kitchen to throw it away. My blood pressure was skyrocketing! What the hell did I get involved in this time? I had never had a cat do this to me before—I was starting to think that Machi ending up in the shelter was almost inevitable!

The *litter!* I had a light bulb moment. Maybe he didn't like the *litter*. So I had some of the regular litter that Emily had given to us. I poured out the Feline Pine and replaced it with the regular litter. Sal took Machi and placed him in the box and instantly, he pooped. We were like two morons standing there rejoicing that this big cat was pooping in the litter box! That was the problem. Machi is not a Feline Pine guy! Who knew? He likes that regular, yucky stuff that I hate, but have never been so happy to use!

A little over a week passed, and it looked like Machi was a keeper. He was affectionate and claimed my dining room window sill as his throne. He even seemed to be comfortable in our home. He hadn't had any accidents and was eating like the big fellow he is!

A few months after Machi's arrival, I brought home a three week old kitten. She was solid black right down to her paw pads. We called her Screamin Mimi because when she was hungry she was a Screamin Mimi. After we weaned "*Screami*," we started to let her walk around the house a little. That's when we got the biggest surprise of our lives. Machi loved her. Machi was huge compared to her—Screami was less than one pound. She was so young that she had no fear in her and hadn't learned to hiss. She followed Machi around and made sure to become his best friend. The way they interacted was beyond words. She followed him everywhere, and he taught her to climb, hide and play. We even caught him grooming her one day. They were inseparable. Sal was starting to say that we had to keep Screami for Machi and that Machi would be so sad when we gave her away. But I did not need another cat! We kept Screami for about four weeks and during that time we watched them play under the covers that were on the furniture, run through the entire length of the house like two psychos, skidding as they tried to make the turns at the doorways. We watched Screami run straight towards Machi and then run under him from front to back. He was a gentle giant with her, and we could see that he was happy to have a little friend to play with. When we placed Screami, I felt very guilty about taking away Machi's friend.

During the last week of fostering Screami, we took in two other kitties, and we were fostering them downstairs. We called them Lenny and Squiggy. They were two little orange kitties that were brought to me from someone on the other side of Brooklyn. How they heard about me is a mystery, but, once we had gotten Screami a home, we moved Lenny and Squiggy upstairs to have Machi interact with them. They were very insecure kittens and needed all the help they could get in terms of getting socialized and building confidence. So, here comes Machi to the rescue. After a little initial hissing and spitting, it turned out that Machi loved these guys too! At first the kittens were terrified of this gentle giant kitty! Machi seemed a little hesitant to be their friend because there were two of them. But as Machi watched them play with each other, he decided that he didn't want to be left out and so he began to play with them. Machi enjoyed having these little fellows around to play with, and we now consider Machi to be our "socializer."

NOW WHAT?

REAT QUESTION! THIS book chronicled a little over the first year of my mission. Believe it or not, there were probably twice as many stories that were not told. That's *how many* animals were helped in that whirlwind time. As you saw, it was an emotional roller-coaster of a year but certainly the most rewarding of my life. The purpose of this book is not to exhaust or overwhelm anyone but rather to inspire and encourage. Look at what can be accomplished by a group of animal loving people in a small community. As of this final editing, we have saved 636 pets from death in two years. *Anyone* can do it! You just have to be willing to put the time and energy into this desperate cause, but the rewards are rich and the friendships you will make are stronger than any other.

I hope that as you read this book you got to know me and my own pets. Anyone who is lucky enough to compliment their home with a furry friend or two probably could see themselves and their pet in some of my stories. I believe that we are blessed with the ability to love an animal the way it deserves to be loved. Without you even realizing it, this gift empowers you to take the next step. While it may seem daunting to get something like this off the ground, you will be pleasantly surprised to see that you're surrounded by animal loving people who have been waiting for the opportunity to arise to help these pets. My volunteers are people like you and me. Animal lovers who desperately want to help but, for whatever reason, can't get themselves to the shelter to offer it. By taking my approach of bringing the shelter to your community, you are not only helping save lives, you are also helping your fellow man fulfill his or her potential to make an important and rewarding difference.

When you read the statistics and come to terms with the harsh reality that scores of kill shelters euthanize, in many cases, more pets than they are able to place each week, it should serve as an alarm clock blaring at full volume. Your desire to change this reality should strongly increase. The bottom line is that despite having wonderful, tremendously dedicated people staffing these over-burdened shelters, they desperately need and want our help. Please take my words and ideas and put them to good use. Become part of the solution. Stop standing by the sidelines lamenting over how sad things are. Instead, use your blessing of being an animal lover to change those ugly statistics in your neighborhood, today! Each day you wait, more lives are lost! It all begins with a phone call. Pick up the phone and reach out to your local shelter today. Simply offer to HELP, like I did! The rest will be history.

Know that every cause deserves a "village." Every community has a "village" within. It just requires someone taking the first step in discovering it. Why not be that someone?